Lake District
Eastern Lakeland

Walks

Compiled by
Terry Marsh

Text:	Terry Marsh
Photography:	Terry Marsh
Editorial:	Ark Creative (UK) Ltd
Design:	Ark Creative (UK) Ltd

ISBN 978-1-85458-499-1

While every care has been taken to ensure the accuracy of the route directions, the publishers cannot accept responsibility for errors or omissions, or for changes in details given. The countryside is not static: hedges and fences can be removed, field boundaries can alter, footpaths can be rerouted and changes in ownership can result in the closure or diversion of some concessionary paths. Also, paths that are easy and pleasant for walking in fine conditions may become slippery, muddy and difficult in wet weather, while stepping stones across rivers and streams may become impassable.

If you find an inaccuracy in either the text or maps, please write to Crimson Publishing at the address below.

First published in Great Britain 2009 by Crimson Publishing, a division of:
Crimson Business Ltd,
Westminster House, Kew Road, Richmond, Surrey, TW9 2ND

www.totalwalking.co.uk

Printed in Singapore. 1/09

A catalogue record for this book is available from the British library.

Front cover: Tewet Tarn
Previous page: Brothers Water

Contents

Contents

Approximate walk times

 Up to 2 hours   2½–3½ hours   4 hours and over

The walk times are provided as a guide only and are calculated using an average walking speed of 2½mph (4km/h), adding one minute for each 10m (33ft) of ascent, and then rounding the result to the nearest half hour.

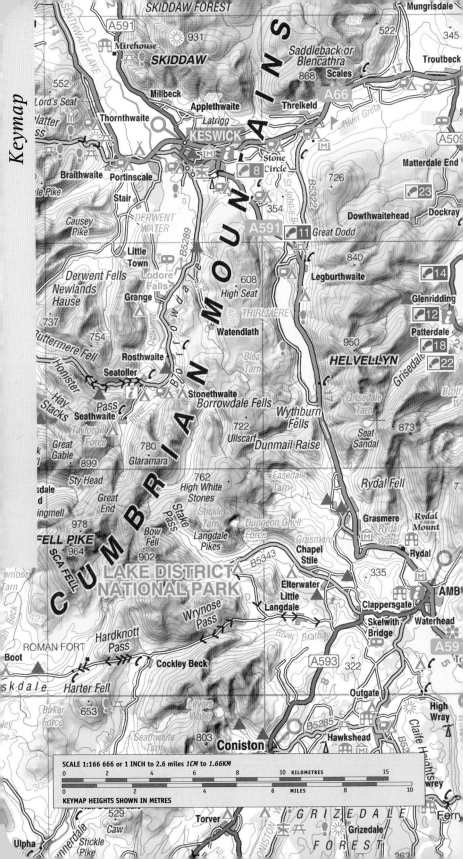

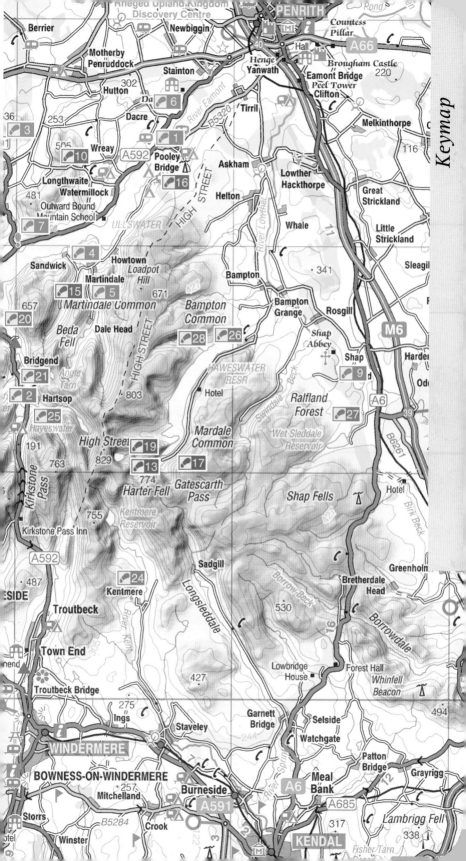

Keymap

At-a-glance...

Walk	Page	Start	Nat. Grid Reference	Distance	Time	Height Gain
Adam Seat and Harter Fell	42	Mardale Head	NY 469107	4½ miles (7km)	2½ hrs	1,755ft (535m)
Aira Force and Gowbarrow Park	25	Patterdale	NY 401201	4 miles (6.5km)	2 hrs	1,253ft (382m)
Angle Tarn and Hayeswater	63	Hartsop	NY 403134	8 miles (12.5km)	4½ hrs	2,310ft (705m)
Beda Fell	47	Martindale	NY 433190	5½ miles (9km)	3 hrs	1,510ft (460m)
Branstree and Selside Pike	53	Mardale Head	NY 469107	5½ miles (9.2km)	3 hrs	1,740ft (530m)
Brotherswater	14	Hartsop	NY 403134	2¼ miles (3.75km)	1 hr	230ft (70m)
Castlerigg and Tewet Tarn	28	Castlerigg	NY 292237	4 miles (6.5km)	2 hrs	655ft (200m)
Dalemain and Dacre	22	Dalemain	NY 477270	4½ miles (7.25km)	2 hrs	445ft (135m)
Dunmallard Hill	12	Pooley Bridge	NY 469245	2 miles (3km)	1 hr	345ft (105m)
Glenridding and Lanty's Tarn	39	Glenridding	NY 386169	5¼ miles (8.3km)	2½ hrs	1,015ft (310m)
Great Dodd and Clough Head	69	High Row, Dockray	NY 380219	8¼ miles (13.2km)	4½ hrs	2,035ft (620m)
Great Mell Fell	16	Matterdale End	NY407247	2 miles (3.5km)	1½ hrs	855ft (260m)
Grisedale	56	Patterdale	NY 396159	7 miles (11km)	3½ hrs	1,280ft (390m)
Hallin Fell	18	Martindale	NY 435192	3 miles (4.5km)	1½ hrs	690ft (210m)
Hartsop Round	77	Hartsop	NY 403134	8 miles (12.7km)	4½ hrs	2,560ft (780m)
Haweswater shore path	80	Burnbanks	NY 508161	10 miles (16.3km)	4½ hrs	1,273ft (388m)
Helvellyn	66	Patterdale	NY 396159	8¼ miles (13.2km)	5 hrs	3,165ft (965m)
High Rigg and St John's in the Vale	36	Legburthwaite	NY 318195	5 miles (8km)	2½ hrs	1,215ft (370m)
Kentmere Round	72	Kentmere	NY 456041	13 miles (21km)	7 hrs	3,805ft (1,160m)
Little Mell Fell	34	Thackthwaite	NY 417252	4¼ miles (6.75km)	2½ hrs	1,065ft (325m)
Loadpot Hill to High Raise	88	Burnbanks	NY 508161	14½ miles (23.5km)	7½ hrs	3,280ft (1,000m)
Pikeawassa	20	Martindale	NY 434184	3 miles (4.5km)	1½ hrs	950ft (290m)
Place Fell	60	Patterdale	NY 396159	7 miles (11.5km)	4 hrs	2,265ft (690m)
Pooley Bridge and Barton Park	50	Pooley Bridge	NY 469245	6 miles (9.5km)	3 hrs	770ft (235m)
Rough Crag and High Street	58	Mardale Head	NY 469107	5½ miles (9km)	3½ hrs	2,100ft (640m)
Shap Abbey	31	Shap	NY 563151	4½ miles (7.5km)	2 hrs	425ft (130m)
Sheffield Pike and Glenridding Dodd	44	Glencoynedale	NY 386189	5 miles (8km)	3 hrs	1,935ft (590m)
Wet Sleddale, Swindale and Mosedale	84	Wet Sleddale	NY 555114	12½ miles (17.5km)	5½ hrs	1,540ft (470m)

Comments

A roundabout route to arguably the finest view of Mardale and Haweswater, linking two mountain passes, and a fine outing across two high fells.

A popular visit to one of Lakeland's finest waterfalls, but bolted on to a heady exploration of the craggy upland of Gowbarrow Fell above; concluding with a fine terraced path across steep fell slopes.

A brief jaunt with part of the Coast-to-Coast walk across the fells above Patterdale, returning by the shores of an isolated and idyllic tarn, and the rustic hamlet of Hartsop.

A splendid ridge walk high above Boredale and Bannerdale, culminating in a retreat through the latter; a peaceful and remote outing.

Climbing steadily from the remote head of Mardale, the walk finds the easiest way onto Branstree to begin an easy and delightful amble across moorland tops.

An easy amble in the footsteps of Dorothy Wordsworth beside a lovely lake to an ancient hall, seat of the Earls of Lonsdale. Flora and fauna is exceptional at most times of year.

Arguably Britain's finest stone circle, Castlerigg is a key Lakeland feature, here combined with a romp across farmland to the northern end of a bumpy ridge leading to a secluded church.

There is so much history, antiquity and intrigue soaked into this walk there almost isn't enough time to do the walk.

A brief outing to a fine conical hill and Iron Age fort site overlooking Ullswater. The walk continues across farmland to the north before making a return alongside the River Eamont.

Launching itself from the tourist hotspot of Glenridding, the walk visits the site of the largest lead mine in the Lake District, before skipping southwards into Grisedale, by way of secluded Lanty's Tarn.

In spite of an apparently easy profile and gentle going, the Dodds offer some of the most demanding moorland walking in the region. This walk makes good use of an ancient highway to gain the fells.

An easy, if steep, ascent to an isolated fell of some geological uniqueness; steep descents tend to discourage continuation across the fell. A straightforward up-and-down stroll will prove rewarding enough.

Sandwiched between St Sunday Crag and Striding Edge, Grisedale tends to be overlooked. Saunter up this delightful dale, increasingly rugged and with high fells all around.

A simple circuit of a splendid little fell with a grandstand view across the lake of Ullswater. A chance to visit the east side of Patterdale.

Climbing to the highest of the eastern fells, this walk leads you in by a less familiar route that offers a surprise view and an outstanding high-level circuit.

Although an entirely low-level walk, this circuit of Haweswater can be tiring. It uses a section of the popular Coast-to-Coast walk, and makes a splendid round for a long summer's day.

A demanding, scrambly route along Lakeland's most renowned ridge leads to the high plateau-like summit of Helvellyn before making an awkward descent to a wild amphitheatre containing Red Tarn.

High Rigg is a delightful, undulating ridge largely ignored by walkers, other than a discerning few. Numerous nooks and crannies offer shelter.

A long and ambitious circuit of the delectable Kent Valley, maintaining a high level throughout in more ways than one. A cut-out at the halfway stage allows for a speedy return to the start if needed.

A surprisingly delightful romp along country lanes and across an isolated fell with an interesting geological history.

A significant undertaking, rising high onto the rounded fells between Mardale and Martindale to the west. The walk concludes by following the east-bound Coast-to-Coast walk alongside Haweswater.

A splendid and simple romp across a little-known fell at the heart of Martindale on the east side of Ullswater.

Looming above the eastern side of Ullswater, Place Fell is most often walked around than over; yet it offers superb views and is an exhilarating and energetic walk.

A lazy exploration along the shores of Ullswater and of the fells along its north-eastern flanks, rising onto open moorland inhabited by prehistoric man.

A fine bumpy ridge rises steadily to the base of High Street from where a long pull leads onto the summit plateau. Easy strolling follows as the route descends to Mardale Ill Bell.

A simple enough walk, but imbued with considerable historical interest, which contrasts remarkably with the breezy openness of the moors of Ralfland Forest of old.

A splendid walk through a secluded dale to an oft-neglected summit and neighbouring satellite, both of which provide outstanding views. The walk concludes through Mossdale, and a walk beside Ullswater.

A long and delightful circuit of the moors of Ralfland Forest, visiting remote dales and the location of a cult film.

At-a-glance...

Introduction to the Lake District

The early visitors to the Lake District ventured here with a measure of fear and excitement, not knowing for certain what to expect. Early explorers – Celia Fiennes, Daniel Defoe, Thomas Pennant, Thomas Gray – all described the landscape in various ways, striking a nice (but probably unintentional) balance between description that was inviting and text that proved a deterrent. We know there were no dragons in the Lake District, nor is it suggested that anyone ever seriously thought there were. But many visitors believed there was mischief and ill-fortune awaiting anyone who ventured too far from the beaten track. Thomas Gray himself, a much- and unfairly maligned travel writer, arguably one of Britain's best, declined to venture all the way down Borrowdale to Seatoller and beyond for fear of what lay there, basing that fear on tales spun by local people. When you recognise that the way down Borrowdale and by way of Styhead into Wasdale is an ancient packhorse route, in use at the time of Gray's visits, and couple that with the certainty that parts of the fells were used for smuggling and illicit whisky distilling, it begs the question that there was a certain amount of codswallop veiling the Lakeland fells.

Yet the dread of mountains persisted for some time, although things were soon to change. John Taylor, the so-called 'Water Poet' (who journeyed on foot from London to Edinburgh and beyond, and described the experience in Penniless Pilgrimage), felt the pull of the mountains. And did so at a time when the norm was still to look on mountainous areas with a fearful eye, as did, for example, Daniel Defoe, who described Westmoreland (sic) as being 'a country eminent only for being the wildest, most barren and frightful of any that I have passed over in England, or even in Wales it self; the west side, which borders on Cumberland, is indeed bounded by a chain of almost unpassable mountains, which, in the language of the country, are called Fells.'

In spite of these claims – and there is some doubt that Defoe ever got farther north than Lancaster – people seem to have been climbing Skiddaw, at least, for some centuries. Bishop Nicolson of Carlisle, for example, went up with friends as early as 1684 ... for the mere pleasure of going there, which Ruskin's secretary, W. G. Collingwood notes '... seems to have been a well-known point of view.'

But quite when the modern cult of walking took off is not certain. The Victorians, keen on exploration and appreciation of the landscape, certainly came to the Lakes in large numbers, especially after the arrival of the railways in the mid-19th century. Captain Joseph Budworth rambled through the Lakes in 1792 and 1795, covering more than 240 miles. Unaffected by the prevailing Romantic mood, he walked freely among the fells and 'trundled

Heron

boulders down Helvellyn', doing so for the experience and to enjoy himself. What is remarkable about his accounts of walking in the Lake District is the appealing frankness, which caused him to confess his own inadequacy as when he bandaged up one eye before crossing the fell slopes below Langdale Pikes, in order not to see what lay below. Budworth's ascent of the Old Man of Coniston is often cited as the first 'tourist' ascent of the mountain. That was barely 200 years ago, and as we romp the fells today it is difficult to imagine what it might have felt like to make the first, or, at least, the first recorded, exploration of the fells.

Wordsworth and the so-called Lake Poets are generally credited (or blamed, depending on your point of view), for bringing increasing numbers of tourists to the Lake District. That is neither entirely true nor fair, other writers were here before them. But Wordsworth lived in the Lake District and knew it intimately, and certain it is that his descriptive writings did much to attract visitors. Even so, the vogue for personal narratives masquerading as guidebooks went on well into the 19th century, most written on the basis of brief tours by outsiders. They were significant in creating a literary illusion, leaving little to the individual's imagination, directing their appreciation of the landscape rather than influencing or persuading independent exploration and discovery. What made the work of Wordsworth, Harriet Martineau and

William Green so different, and therefore valuable, is that they lived here, and knew the region intimately.

The Lake District today is all things to all men (and women). Each visitor sees the Lakeland landscape in a different way. Some describe the fells, others the dales, the rivers, lakes, tarns and meres. There are many landscape features, but overall, in a physical sense, it is the fells and the lakes that are the key to the region's popularity. And although water appears throughout the length and breadth of Britain, in the Lake District it is the presence of so much water in such a compact area set among dramatic fells and beautiful dales, themselves bounded north, west and south by even greater expanses of water, that makes this region so remarkably different from other parts of Britain, and so palpably unique – the 'Odd Corner of England' as it has been called.

Nor can it be overlooked that the Lake District comprises the only significant mountainous region in England, uniquely distinctive, so much so that the National Park Authority was able to adopt as its emblem the arrangement of fells at the head of Wasdale, arguably the most inaccessible

High Rigg Tarn, and Clough Head

dale for the vast majority of visitors. Yet it is a landscape arrangement at once symbolic, iconic and instantly recognisable.

Eastern Lakeland

No attempt to corral fells into meaningful groups can ever be wholly satisfactory; the Lake District simply does not lend itself to being parcelled. But in this eastern collection of walks, the reader is invited to explore not only some of the more populous areas, but those that are less well known, but no less delectable a part of the District.

There is a measure of definition to this particular group: it is bounded on the east by the A6 at Shap, in the north by the A66, the Penrith to Keswick road. Towards the west, the A591 has been taken as a boundary, mainly because that unashamedly allows for the inclusion of a walk from Castlerigg stone circle, as well as along the splendid High Rigg ridge overlooking St John's in the Vale. It is to the south that the dividing line is less convincing, but generally swings eastwards from Dunmail Raise to the Kirkstone Pass and then all things eastwards.

Walks to the west of Patterdale are quite well known, especially those that launch from Glenridding. But farther north, Gowbarrow Fell, and the two Mell Fells and the exquisite countryside around Dacre and Dalemain, offer the most splendid walking. The east side of Ullswater, reached by a very long cul-de-sac, lends itself to much quieter exploration with the ridge of Beda Fell surely one of Lakeland's gems. But the opportunity has been taken, too, to visit the moorland expanses of the Shap Fells and the remote valleys of Swindale and Mosedale, places where you can walk and savour the companionship of solitude in abundance.

This is a far from perfect menu, made all the more deficient by what has had to be left out, but there is a fair balance between familiar and less familiar, sufficient at least to bring joy to everyone who loves the Lakeland fells. To detail every summit in the Lake District takes many volumes, as a number of authors have demonstrated; to do them all justice must surely defeat everyone, for there is just too much, too many details, so much history, intrigue, fascination and unadulterated joy.

This book includes a list of waypoints alongside the description of the walk, so that you can enjoy the full benefits of gps should you wish to. For more information on using your gps, read the *Pathfinder® Guide GPS for Walkers*, by gps teacher and navigation trainer, Clive Thomas (ISBN 978-0-7117-4445-5). For essential information on map reading and basic navigation, read the *Pathfinder® Guide Map Reading Skills* by outdoor writer, Terry Marsh (ISBN 978-0-7117-4978-8). Both titles are available in bookshops or can be ordered online at www.totalwalking.co.uk

Dunmallard Hill

		GPS waypoints
Start	Pooley Bridge	
Distance	2 miles (3km)	NY 469 245
Height gain	345 feet (105m)	Ⓐ NY 467 246
		Ⓑ NY 468 248
Approximate time	1 hour	Ⓒ NY 471 249
Parking	Pooley Bridge (Pay and Display)	
Route terrain	Woodland; farmland	
Ordnance Survey maps	Landranger 90 (Penrith & Keswick), Explorer OL5 (The English Lakes – North-eastern area)	

This brief introduction to walking in Patterdale is remarkably popular, climbing as it does to a viewpoint (now rather obscured) that was popular with the Victorian visitors who came in search of enlightenment.

Go to the road edge of the car park at Pooley Bridge, and through a gate on the right, taking a circular route around Dunmallard Hill (ignore the path for Dacre). The path sets off just above the road, but then climbs gently, and, at a point above the pier, the path forks. Keep right, still climbing gently on a clear path, that circles around the hill, almost to its northern side, where you meet a path descending from the right.

Turn right up the path and follow this to the wooded summit of Dunmallard Hill Ⓐ. There is little to see of the lake, other than in winter, as the trees obscure much of the view. But it is an historic location and the effort required

Dunmallard Hill

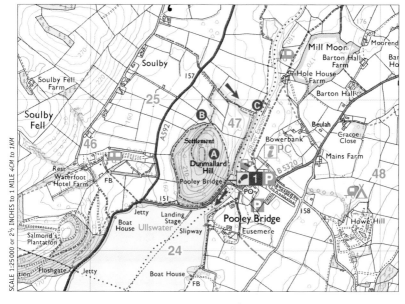

is not excessive.

Dunmallard Hill, shrouded in trees, conceals a small and undistinguished Iron Age hill fort. Cleric Thomas West in his *Guide to the Lakes,* which went through many editions, listed a series of 'stations' from which to best observe the landscape and scenery of the Lakes. Dunmallard Hill (Dunmallet in West's

guide) was not one of the original stations, but was added after his death and is shown on Peter Crosthwaite's charming 1794 map of Ullswater as 'West's First Station'.

James Clarke in his monumental *Survey of the Lakes* first published in 1787, intriguingly records 'Upon the top of Dunmallard was a Monastery of Benedictines', but qualifies it with a footnote suggesting that 'This must certainly be the monastery mentioned by Bede ... to have been at Dacre.'

Return to the lower path and follow it a little farther to a stile **B** giving access to a sloping field to the north. Descend to cross an intermediate fence from which you bear diagonally left to a stile at the end of a wall. Over this, you join a bridleway. Now turn right beside the fence and walk as far as a step-stile by a gate. Cross this and continue down beside the fence, walking towards the River Eamont. Just above the river **C**, turn right and walk towards the base of Dunmallard Hill woodland where you pass through a gate and on to a fine riverside path that takes you back to the start. ●

Brotherswater

Start	Hartsop	GPS waypoints	
Distance	2¼ miles (3.75km)	🏁	NY 403 134
Height gain	230 feet (70m)	Ⓐ	NY 398 120
		Ⓑ	NY 404 120
Approximate time	1 hour	Ⓒ	NY 405 130
Parking	Cow Bridge		
Route terrain	Woodland; lakeside paths		
Ordnance Survey maps	Landranger 90 (Penrith & Keswick), Explorer OL5 (The English Lakes – North-eastern area)		

Although of itself not unduly spectacular, Brothers Water facilitates a delightful and relaxing amble through woodland that is especially rich in birdlife, and by the shores of the lake, which in summer are coloured by rafts of water lilies.

Brothers Water

🏁 Leave the car park and cross the nearby bridge spanning Goldrill Beck, and turn left through a gate giving onto a broad, stony track. The track, never far from water, runs along the bottom edge of well-established oak and beech, Low Wood, wherein many species of bird delight.

Dorothy Wordsworth, having left William sitting on Cow Bridge, walked through Low Wood on April 16, 1802, delighted with '... the boughs of the bare old trees, the simplicity of the mountains, and the exquisite beauty of the path ... the gentle flowing of the stream, the glittering, lively lake, green fields without a living creature to be seen on them.'

Gradually, the path rises gently, pulling away from the water's edge, and, beyond the southern end of the lake, continues above broad alluvial pastures to reach Hartsop Hall Ⓐ and Dovedale Cottage.

Hartsop Hall was built originally in the 16th century, though it has been extensively rebuilt and altered since. It was formerly the home of the de Lancasters, and later of Sir John Lowther, who became the first Viscount Lonsdale at the end of the 17th century. When the hall was extended in the 18th century, it was built across an ancient right of way, a right which at least one dalesman insisted on exercising, by walking through the hall.

Follow the track past the hall and, ignoring paths going off to the right, swing round to the left, in front of the hall, and then follow a track, right, over a cattle-grid and walk along a level track towards a caravan and camping site at Sykeside Farm.

Sykeside Farm was the home of 'Old Charlie Dixon', a local shepherd, who died there in 1936 at the age of 83. Charlie never left the Lake District, yet he became world famous; he was the original shepherd in many of the most famous pastoral photographs ever taken. *The Shepherd and the Lost Sheep* and *A Westmorland Shepherd* are lost to modern digital generations, but revered by photographers for whom the Box Brownie was the cutting edge of contemporary photography.

Continue through the site on a surfaced track, and go past the shop and other buildings, bearing left at a Y-junction near the **Brothers Water Hotel.** Follow a driveway until, just as it reaches the road, leave it for a gate on

the left giving on to a permissive path **B** signposted for Brothers Water.

Initially the path hugs the road wall, and soon reaches a gap where, for a few strides, it adjoins the road. Then it descends to the shoreline of Brothers Water.

The lake was once called Broad Water, but it was changed in the 19th century after two brothers had drowned there.

At various spots here the shoreline would be an ideal place for a picnic. In summer the water surface is carpeted with lilies.

Gradually the path leaves the waterside and rises to a gate **C** giving access to the road. Turn left and cross to a footpath opposite, and follow the road back to the Cow Bridge car park at the start of the walk. ●

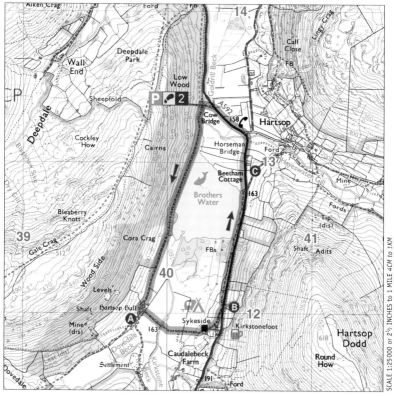

Great Mell Fell

		GPS waypoints
Start	Near Matterdale End	 NY 407 247
Distance	2 miles (3.5km)	Ⓐ NY 405 245
Height gain	855 feet (260m)	Ⓑ NY 401 250
Approximate time	1½ hours (*variant 1*), 2 hours (*variant 2*)	
Parking	Limited roadside parking at start	
Route terrain	Woodland track, open, grassy fellside	
Ordnance Survey maps	Landranger 90 (Penrith & Keswick), Explorer OL5 (The English Lakes – North-eastern area)	

The conquest of Great Mell Fell should faze no one; the fell is a simple, rounded dome, easy and delightful of access. Walk 10, which visits neighbouring Little Mell Fell, contains information about the unique geological make-up of these two isolated fells, although it is less easy to make a circular walk on the higher of the two without making a very steep descent at some stage. Even so, a straightforward amble to the top and back will be found quite sufficiently rewarding. The two Mell Fells will never compete with the Scafells, Skiddaw or Helvellyn for walkers' attention, but there is a smug satisfaction about having added them both to the list of Lakeland fells completed.

The walk begins at a rough track leaving the road not far from Brownrigg Farm. Set off along the track, and continue past a National Trust Mell Fell

Great Mell Fell

sign at a gate, as this is not the way to go, in spite of it being rather inviting.

Stay on the stony track as far as the next gate on the right Ⓐ. Pass through the gate and then bear left alongside a fence, climbing gently. For a while the path is flanked on the right by trees, but as these finally fall back you can leave the fence-side path by branching right onto a steeply ascending path.

A brief, leg-buckling climb soon eases a little, but the ascent continues, climbing past a number of wind-blown trees, and rising clearly through bracken. Eventually, you come on to the end of a very broad and rounded ridge. Here, swing left, still ascending but now more gently towards the left-hand edge of woodland.

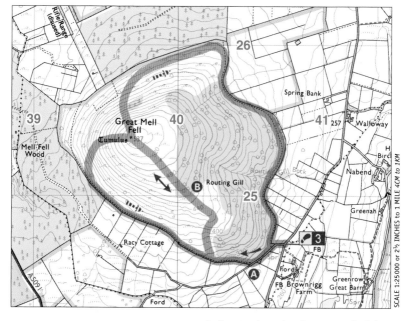

SCALE 1:25000 or 2½ INCHES to 1 MILE 4CM to 1KM

```
0      200    400    600    800 METRES   1
                                          KILOMETRES
                                          MILES
0      200    400    600 YARDS   ½
```

before too long, leaving you to find the easiest gradient.

The path now above the bracken appears to lead directly into the trees, but then as you gain more height it bears left and passes through the end of the woodland **B**, mainly of Scots pine and larch. There is a fine view across Matterdale to the Dodds.

Just as you finally approach the summit, Blencathra eases into view. The top of Great Mell Fell is marked by a small cairn within a collapsed tumulus and on a fine day this is a truly wonderful place to be.

The surest return is now to retrace your steps because by any other route only very steep descents on grass (slippery when wet) await. Even so, those with the ability to deal with descents of this kind can add a little distance to the day.

Variant routes
From the top of Great Mell Fell, two indistinct grassy paths set off one roughly in a northerly direction, and the other roughly to the west. Both fade

1. *If you go west, the slope gradually steepens considerably, finally descending through gorse and bracken to reach a clear track running along the edge of Mell Fell Wood (partially cleared). Once the track is underfoot, simply turn left (south-east) and follow it back to the start. This option will add less than 200 yds to the overall walking distance.*

2. *If you decide to go north, then an equally steep descent awaits, also to the boundary of woodland, but this time there is no path of any note to reassure you. When you do reach the woodland boundary, simply turn right (north-east) and follow it almost to the eastern edge of the woodland where a good path is then encountered. Turn right (south) onto this, and take its sinuous course around the base of Great Mell Fell finally emerging at the National Trust sign encountered in the early stages of the walk. This option will increase the overall distance to 3 miles, with 940ft (335m) of height gain.* ●

Hallin Fell

		GPS waypoints
Start	Martindale	🥾 NY 435 192
Distance	3 miles (4.5km), including Hallin Fell top 3¾ miles (6km)	Ⓐ NY 433 204
Height gain	690 feet (210m), including Hallin Fell top 1,180 feet (360m)	Ⓑ NY 426 199
		Ⓒ NY 426 193
Approximate time	1½ hours, *variant route* 2 hours	
Parking	Martindale	
Route terrain	Rocky paths; field paths, a little road walking	
Ordnance Survey maps	Landranger 90 (Penrith & Keswick), Explorer OL5 (The English Lakes – North-eastern area)	

The east side of Ullswater has a tendency to be shunned by many walkers, mainly because of the difficulty of getting there. It's either a long drive down a narrow road from Pooley Bridge to the head of Martindale, or a trip across the lake on one of the steamers, with all the attendant concern about missing the last boat back.

🥾 As you approach Howtown, the hitherto mundane road decides to become alpine, and sweeps upwards in zigzags with benches placed at strategic locations so that walkers can watch motorists getting into difficulty. Eventually, you pass through a narrow gap between Hallin Fell and Steel Knotts, the summit of which delights in the name Pikeawassa. Just over the high point, there's a car park opposite St Peter's Church.

Martindale to the south holds a lot of interest; archaeological studies in the area have shown settlements here dating from the Bronze Age, through Roman times and into the Middle Ages – the Roman 'High Street' crosses the felltops to the east.

The walk is circular, and simply tours Hallin Fell; the only decision you have to make is whether to climb to the summit first, when you get back, or not at all. The view from the obelisk-like

cairn on the summit is stunning, with the length of Ullswater rippling away to the north-east. The route description for the ascent to Hallin Fell top is easy: go up, and then come down; there are numerous grassy paths to choose from, that on the left is the most direct. It is well worth the effort to bag this prized summit, which is a Marilyn for those who want to bag summits. The best advice is to do it first.

But to undertake a circuit of Hallin Fell set off northwards, walking initially up the road to the high point, beyond which you can branch left onto a clear path that gradually descends as it heads towards Ullswater, first reaching an inlet of the lake – Howtown Wyke. As you descend, so eventually the path clearly bears left above the wyke, to follow a delightful and unambiguous course to Geordie's Crag and Kailpot Crag, just beyond which you enter Hallinhag Wood Ⓐ, a particularly

Hallin Fell

favoured spot for red squirrels.

Hallinhag Wood is lovely at any time of year, and produces numerous vignettes of Lakeland scenes with distant fells that are constantly changing. You pass Sandwick Bay **B**

before going through gates to follow a clear route out to the hamlet of Sandwick, an indication of the former Scandinavian presence here, as the name is Old Norse, *Sand Vik,* meaning a sandy inlet.

When you reach the end of the road at Beckside Farm, turn left and follow it for about 550 yds, to a branching track **C** on the left, over a bridge at Doe Green, spanning Boredale Beck. A short way farther on, you cross Sandwick Beck by another bridge, and immediately go right to walk along the stream.

The view to the south takes in Boredale and Martindale, with the craggy ridge leading up to Beda Fell making a very attractive profile. A little farther on, as you enter a sloping pasture, follow a green track that sweeps across the fall of the slope to Hallin Bank, and then simply keep on, by stiles and gates, until you finally return to the starting point.

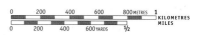

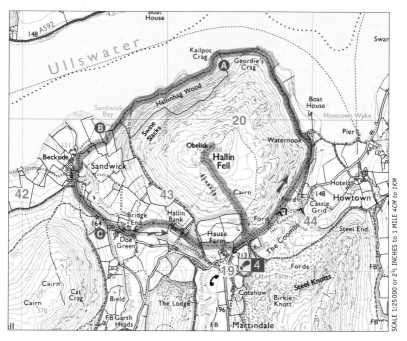

SCALE 1:25000 or 2½ INCHES to 1 MILE 4CM to 1KM

Pikeawassa

Start	Martindale	**GPS waypoints**	
Distance	3 miles (4.5km)	🥾 NY 434 184	
Height gain	950 feet (290m)	Ⓐ NY 439 178	
Approximate time	1½ hours	Ⓑ NY 443 194	
Parking	Martindale church	Ⓒ NY 435 190	
Route terrain	Open fell slopes and ridge; rocky outcrops; steep descent		
Ordnance Survey maps	Landranger 90 (Penrith & Keswick), Explorer OL5 (The English Lakes – North-eastern area)		

Strictly speaking Pikeawassa is the name of the rocky upthrust that marks the top of a low, steep-sided ridge, Steel Knotts, lying between the valleys of Martindale and Fusedale. The ridge is also known as Martindale Edge, and is essentially a subsidiary spur from Wether Hill, one of the great rounded fells to the east. This brief sortie should tax no one, yet delight everyone who sets foot upon its slopes. Pikeawassa suits an ambling, lazy half day, in winter maybe, or when time is pressing. But of all the summits to the east of Ullswater, this diminutive fell is just too good to miss, and could easily be approached by using the steamer service from Glenridding – but do check the return pick-up times; it's a long walk back if you miss the last ferry.

🥾 There is room to park cars off road near the old church of St Martin's, which originates in the 16th century,

Martindale old church: the start of the ascent to Pikeawassa goes up the grooved hillside in the background

and from here you begin by passing to the left of the churchyard. At the back, a broad green track sets off in a south-easterly direction, but ignore this in favour of a more direct, more easterly ascent of a shallow groove rising between a couple of wide-spaced boulders, and climbing quickly to intercept a higher track.

Once on the higher track simply turn right and follow this across the fall of slope until you meet a wall Ⓐ above Nettlehowe Crag. You can pass through the wall if you wish and then later double back onto the summit ridge. But it is easier to turn upwards on reaching the wall to gain the ridge – it saves wear and tear on walls.

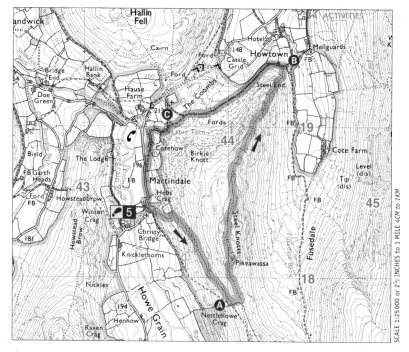

SCALE 1:25000 or 2½ INCHES to 1 MILE 4CM to 1KM

On reaching the ridge, a lovely, mildly undulating romp ensues, running northwards to the craggy top of Pikeawassa, the very summit of which will defeat a few.

After that, it's all downhill, more or less, following a clear path that centres the descending ridge as it bends gently to the east, finally dropping through crags, and steeply, to meet a clear track **B** just above Howtown.

The summit of Pikeawassa from Beda Fell

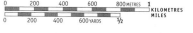

Turn left along the track, climbing steadily now as it rises across the northern slope of Steel Knotts. Eventually, as the track levels and then swings to the right, you can leave it near tiny Lanty Tarn **C** for a path that descends to Cotehow, and then to the road in Martindale. Now just turn left along the road to return to the church at the start. ●

Dalemain and Dacre

Start	Dalemain	**GPS waypoints**	
Distance	4½ miles (7.25km)	✎ NY 477 270	
Height gain	445 feet (135m)	Ⓐ NY 471 257	
		Ⓑ NY 471 249	
Approximate time	2 hours	Ⓒ NY 464 254	
Parking	Dalemain	Ⓓ NY 459 265	
Route terrain	Farmland; some road walking; woodland		
Ordnance Survey maps	Landranger 90 (Penrith & Keswick), Explorer OL5 (The English Lakes – North-eastern area)		

With the kind permission of the owners, this walk begins from Dalemain, heading from there towards Dunmallard Hill (Walk 1), and then skipping across fields to the village of Dacre. It is a short walk, but one laden with an unprecedented amount of history, antiquity and intrigue.

✎ Set off from the car park at Dalemain and follow the main drive out to the road. There turn right, following the road briefly as it crosses Dacre Beck just west of its confluence with the River Eamont. Leave the road at a stile just south of the Dacre Bridge to enter a large pasture.

Dalemain is a largely 18th-century mansion built around an earlier manor and, possibly, a pele tower believed to date from Norman times. The property has remained in the same family since 1680, when Sir Edward Hasell, the son of the rector of Middleton Cheney in Northamptonshire, purchased it from the de Laytons. Sir Edward was secretary to Lady Anne Clifford until her death in 1675, when he settled in Cumberland. He married Jane Fetherstonhaugh of Kirkoswald, and, after sitting as Member of Parliament for Cumberland, was knighted by William III.

Today the mansion is open to visitors, as are the gardens, which have been developed by succeeding generations to provide five acres of richly planted herbaceous borders. Of particular interest to fatigued walkers is the splendid **tearoom** complete with large open fire.

Bear left across the pasture to connect with a broad grassy track leading up to the top corner of Langfield Wood. As you reach the edge of the woodland, walk across to a waymark and then a gate/stile from which you follow a grassy track alongside a fence, directly targeting Dunmallard Hill.

The fenceside path eventually leads down to intercept another at which you can turn left and walk out to the A592 Ⓐ. Cross the road to a verge opposite and turn left. After about 50 yds, turn through a kissing-gate giving on to a footpath for Pooley Bridge. Now walk along the edge of a large field, with a fence on your left.

Soon, the path passes a small lake fringed with bulrush, and runs on along a line of beautiful Lombardy poplar trees. Lombardy poplar trees, which have distinctive upturned branches that form a towering spire, were once regularly planted to adorn driveways and to act as wind breaks. One childhood tale relates that the poplar furls its branches upwards because it was within them that King Charles II sought to escape the Roundheads at the end of the English Civil War in 1651. Of course, that could not have been possible, however delightful a notion, because the Lombardy poplar was not introduced into Britain until 1758 by Lord Rochford, then ambassador to Turin. Tradition has it that it was an oak tree in the grounds of Boscobel House on the border of Shropshire that actually sheltered the fugitive king.

At the end of the line of poplars, cross a step-stile and walk around the end of the lake to a gate in a badly drained corner close by the River Eamont. Now simply parallel the river, heading upstream, with the path crossing the base of a number of fields before reaching a gate **B** entering a field below wooded Dunmallard Hill.

Through the gate turn right, climbing beside a fence until, higher up, you can cross it at a step-stile, and keep alongside it once more until it descends to meet the A592.

Cross the road and go through a gate opposite, and then follow a fence on the left. The fenceside path crosses two fields and eventually climbs to a gate and stile at a narrow lane, adjoining a monumental sycamore tree **C**. Turn right and stroll along the lane to a road

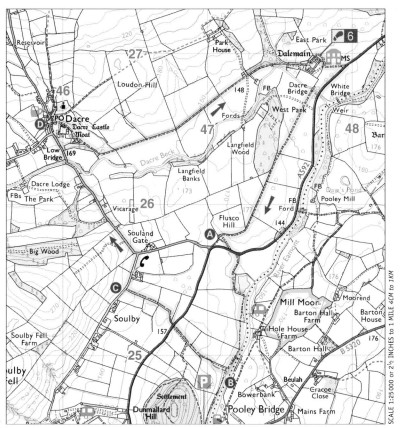

junction, and there turn left walking easily towards the village of Dacre.

As you crest a rise, so Dacre comes into view. A long descent leads down to the village. Cross Dacre Beck and walk uphill to the tiny village green complete with stocks. Opposite this, turn right onto a path **D** that leads to Dacre Castle. However, it is first worth continuing up the road to visit the church. The Church of St Andrew has a Norman west tower and a late 12th-century chancel, and is believed to have been built on the site of the Saxon monastery mentioned by the Venerable Bede in his Ecclesiastical History of 731, as being 'built near the River Dacre'.

Also of interest in the church is the lock on the south door. It is dated 1671, and is one of a number of locks presented by Lady Anne Clifford to those who had shown her particular kindness. The locks were made for Lady Anne by George Dent of Appleby, and cost £1 each.

The church also contains a memorial tablet to Edward Hasell, bearing a kneeling female figure, which is believed to be the only work in the county of Sir Francis Legatt Chantrey (1781-1841), Derbyshire-born English sculptor, famed for his portrait statues and busts.

Of particular intrigue, at the corners of the churchyard stand the enigmatic Dacre Bears, four large sculptures cut in stone, now well weathered, and thought to commemorate the marriage between Thomas de Dacre and Philippa Neville, although their true origin is unknown. The monuments seem to depict an encounter between a bear and a cat: one shows the bear sleeping, then the cat awakens the bear, which seizes the cat, kills it and promptly eats it.

Return to the village green and take the path that leads past Dacre Castle. Like most Cumberland castles, Dacre Castle began life as a pele tower, and was built in the 14th century. In 1354, a licence for a chapel in the castle was granted by Bishop Welton of Carlisle, and a new tower was added in 1485. It was completely renovated by the last Lord Dacre, Earl of Sussex, in the 1680s and in 1716 it was sold to Sir Christopher Musgrave, who in turn transferred it to his son-in-law Edward Hasell of Dalemain. In times of trouble, villagers would take refuge in Dacre Castle, which would have afforded considerable security, with its massive walls and battlements.

Press on past the castle, following a broad farm track that leads across large pastures and becomes a simple stroll that feeds you in to the rear of Dalemain. Turn left through the archway to return to the car park, although a post perambulatory pot of tea and buttered scones may give you time to digest all the history blended into this walk. ●

Dalemain

Aira Force and Gowbarrow Park

Start	Patterdale, south of Dockray	GPS waypoints
Distance	4 miles (6.5km)	🖉 NY 401 201
Height gain	1,253 feet (382m)	Ⓐ NY 399 215
Approximate time	2 hours	Ⓑ NY 414 217
Parking	Aira Force car park at start (Pay and Display)	Ⓒ NY 412 206
Route terrain	Managed parkland; open fell tops; steep slopes	
Ordnance Survey maps	Landranger 90 (Penrith & Keswick), Explorer OL5 (The English Lakes – North-eastern area)	

Drawing its waters from the grassy folds of Deepdale, Aira Force is one of Lakeland's most admired waterfalls, the showpiece of a fine display of cataracts, tumbling water and deep pools. In this walk, a visit to the Force is combined with a wide, sweeping circuit of Gowbarrow Park, formerly a medieval deer park, and retaining stretches of bleak, rock-punctuated moorland dotted with gnarled oak trees. Gowbarrow, inevitably, is ever associated with daffodils, noticed and recorded by Dorothy in her journal in 1802, and later inspiring one of Wordsworth most memorable poems.

🖉 Leave the Aira Force car park by a gate at its northern end, and through an opening near an information panel, to follow a path above Aira Beck. When the path forks, just after having crossed a minor stream, bear left to pass some fine specimens of yew, and, a short way farther on, a money tree – the sort of novelty that is fairly widespread in the Lake District and elsewhere.

The ongoing path climbs steadily, with the beck bustling away below. As you approach the Force, invariably heard before it is seen, you pass a flight of steps down to the base of the main waterfall. Go down to appreciate the falls, but then return to the top of the steps to resume the original route. The

path now leads up and around to a point high above Aira Force, with steps leading down to a bridge spanning the topmost part of the falls.

The whole area around Aira Force is very attractive, and from the bridge above the falls it is easy enough to abandon the longer walk and simply follow paths down the other side that will take you back to the car park. Cross the Force bridge, and take the first path rising briefly on your left, upstream along the true left bank of the beck, but almost immediately quit this by climbing onto a low shoulder on the right, to a path that leads up to a step-stile. Over the stile, take the path swinging to the left.

The summit of Gowbarrow Fell

At another stile you enter light woodland of birch, hazel and oak, and press on across the top of a flight of steps that leads down to a footbridge. Staying on the continuing path through the woodland you arrive at a higher waterfall, High Force; less dramatic than Aira Force below, but nevertheless (literally) a force to be reckoned with, its banks a delightful place for a breather.

Above High Force, the path, now signed for Dockray and Ulcat Row, continues through a wall gap and a little more woodland. Follow this through thinning woodland, passing a wall before reaching open bracken heath. Cross this towards a wall on the far side, but before reaching the wall, turn right to a ladder-stile, to begin a steady pull up onto Gowbarrow Fell Ⓐ.

The ascending path stays close by a wall, and the opportunity should be taken to pause numerous times to take in the view along the length of Ullswater, and across the Dockray dip to the burgeoning fells of Matterdale Common, rising to Great Dodd. Sheffield Pike peers above the top of Watermillock Common.

Eventually, the path moves away from the wall and bears right to climb to the trig pillar of Gowbarrow Fell, now conspicuous on the skyline.

Cross the top of the fell, taking care on what proves to be a slippery descent on the other side, especially after rain. The path continues descending towards a wall beyond which the darkness of Swinburn's Park looms. But before reaching the wall, bear right in a south-easterly direction, following a clear path to reach the ruins of a shooting lodge Ⓑ.

At the lodge you intercept a right of way, and can follow this roughly in a southerly direction as it climbs slightly to cross three streams all feeding into Collierhagg Beck and Ullswater. *This is a superb traverse, but crosses steep slopes that may deter anyone suffering from vertigo,* but which are not generally a problem. When the path divides (indistinctly), take the prominent left branch, dropping a little before swinging right, around a corner with the top of Yew Crag, a cairned viewpoint, in sight, below and to your

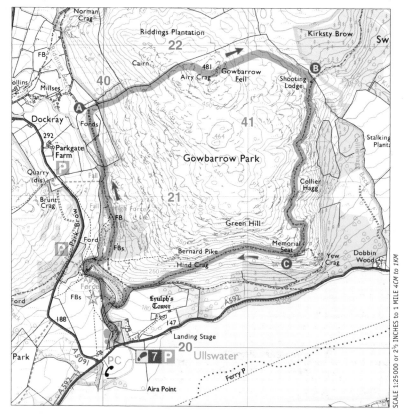

left. Stay above the crag, and pass a memorial seat **C**, then simply follow

SCALE 1:25 000 or 2½ INCHES to 1 MILE 4CM to 1KM

| 0 | 200 | 400 | 600 | 800 METRES | 1 |
| 0 | 200 | 400 | 600 YARDS | ½ | KILOMETRES MILES |

Aira Force

the path, heading steadily downwards, and finally to bear left back into the woodland in the Aira Force grounds just above a noticeable building close by the road below, Lyulph's Tower.

Lyulph's Tower is an 18th-century folly constructed by one of the dukes of Norfolk. It stands on or near the site of the fortress of Lyulph, built by the first Baron Greystoke. Lyulph stems from Ulf, or L'Ulf, Scandinavian for wolf, and leads into Ulf's Water, or Ullswater.

Back within the Aira Force grounds, bear left and take a path that descends to a footbridge. On the other side, climb steps and then bear left, soon to rejoin your outward route, close by the clearing containing yew trees. Simply retrace your steps to the start.

Castlerigg and Tewet Tarn

		GPS waypoints
Start	Castlerigg Stone Circle, Keswick	🥾 NY 292 237
Distance	4 miles (6.5km)	Ⓐ NY 307 238
Height gain	655 feet (200m)	Ⓑ NY 306 224
Approximate time	2 hours	Ⓒ NY 289 225
Parking	Roadside parking area adjoining Castlerigg	
Route terrain	Farmland; low fell country; a little road walking	
Ordnance Survey maps	Landranger 90 (Penrith & Keswick), Explorer OL4 (The English Lakes – North-western area)	

Few visitors reach Keswick without at some stage including a visit to the nearby Castlerigg Stone Circle. It is and has long been a popular place with tourists to the northern Lake District, and rightly so; its ancient stones are a great fascination.
This walk starts and finishes close by Castlerigg, but forms a wide loop to visit reedy Tewet Tarn and the isolated church of St John's in the Vale before trekking back across low-lying farmland.

Castlerigg Stone Circle

Castlerigg is believed to be around 5,000 years old, so pre-dating the great circles at Stonehenge and elsewhere. It is commonly regarded as the most

superb stone circle of the many found in Britain. Enthusiasts believe Castlerigg to be among the earliest stone circles in Europe, though poet John Keats was not impressed, describing the stones (in *Hyperion*) as 'a dismal cirque, Of Druid stones upon a forlorn moor'.

🥾 Leave the stone circle by walking east (away from Keswick) along the lane, but take care against approaching traffic. The road descends round a bend and soon reaches Goosewell Farm. Leave the road by turning through a gate on the right (signposted) and cross to another a short distance away, then head down field diagonally left, aiming for a distant bridge.

Pass through another gate and cross to a ladder-stile at a gate gap, then walk over to a gate giving onto the lane crossing the bridge. Turn right and cross the bridge. Follow the road to a

T-junction and turn right again, walking as far as the next junction on the right (signposted Shundraw and St John's in the Vale Church).

Once more turn right to follow this quiet lane, and again taking care against approaching traffic. After about 385 yds, leave the lane at a five-bar gate on the right **A** (signposted to St John's in the Vale Church via Tewit Tarn). Through the gate, bear right, climbing gently on a grassy vehicle track to reach a wall gap at the top of the field. Beyond the gap continue climbing beside a wall, later bearing away from the wall to a signpost, beyond which Tewet Tarn comes into view.

From the signpost, cross a shallow ravine, and follow an indistinct grassy path across a pasture to a through-stile to the left of a wall gap. Over this, go forward on a broad grassy track to the right of the stile, which passes close by Tewet Tarn.

Set along the northern edge of the undulating ridge of Low Rigg, Tewet (Tewit) Tarn is a small reedy pool set in a hollow, its waters often reflecting Lonscale Fell and Skiddaw to the north. This is a delightfully peaceful setting, far away from the hubbub of towns and busy valley roads.

Once past the tarn, the path improves and heads for a step-stile spanning a fence. Ahead now is Low Rigg, a rugged lump with the highest ground to the south-west, beyond a wall. A grassy path leads towards the slightly lower northern top, and passes just to the right of the summit.

Now the path trundles downhill to cross the wall at a through-stile, after which it continues through bracken, heading for a cluster of buildings in the distance. As the buildings are

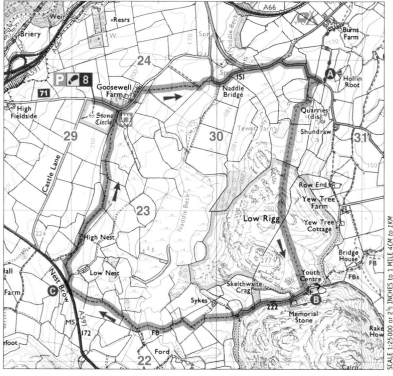

approached, the path picks a way across wet ground to a through-stile giving onto a surfaced lane at St John's in the Vale Church .

The lane, squeezing through a low pass between High Rigg and Low Rigg, was once an important thoroughfare linking the valleys east and west with their church.

The present St John's in the Vale church is Victorian, dating from 1845 with later modifications, though it is thought to incorporate parts of a much earlier, possibly 13th-century, building. It is an unpretentious church, offering a moment of quiet reflection on this walk, and was built to serve the communities that lived in the valleys to either side of the hause on which it is built.

Turn right, pass a Diocesan Youth Centre, and follow the lane to a distant gate. Beyond the gate a broad vehicle track descends, winding down, with widening views, to meet a surfaced lane near Sykes Farm. At this junction, cross to a kissing-gate nearby onto a signposted path. Through the gate walk down-field, following a green path, which soon reaches another gate at the bottom of the field. In the next field, head for a gate on the right at the end

of a wall. Do not go through the gate, but instead keep alongside the ongoing fence to another gate and fence at a wall corner. Beyond this, cross to a nearby footbridge, and cross the next field on a grassy path to a distant signpost at which you encounter a vehicle track.

Turn right, signposted for Keswick, and walk to a gate in a wall corner. Through this continue up the right-hand field margin to a through-stile at the top. Follow a grassy track across the next field to a stile giving onto the busy A591.

Turn right, but 50 yds later, take a right again ⒞ onto an access track to Low Nest Farm. Immediately after crossing a cattle-grid, go left over a step-stile, and walk up the ensuing field on a grassy path that leads to the access to High Nest Farm. Bear right and walk on to pass the farm buildings to a gate, and then keep forward on a muddy path parallel with the right-hand field margin.

Keep to the field margin to reach a kissing-gate. Then cross to another not far away, and repeat this process in the next field, and then follow a green path across rough pasture, heading for a distant plantation of mixed woodland. The path runs past the woodland to meet a lane. Turn left to return to the start. ●

Tewet Tarn

Shap Abbey

		GPS waypoints	
Start	Shap	 NY 563 151	
Distance	4½ miles (7.5km)	**A** NY 545 143	
Height gain	425 feet (130m)	**B** NY 539 152	
Approximate time	2 hours	**C** NY 539 155	
Parking	Shap		
Route terrain	Farmland; moorland; some road walking		
Ordnance Survey maps	Landranger 90 (Penrith & Keswick), Explorer OL5 (The English Lakes – North-eastern area)		

Shap Abbey is a key feature of this walk, a gaunt and evocative ruin on the banks of the River Lowther. But there is more interest besides, not least a huge monolith encountered early in the walk, a small but attractive village and acres of wild moorland where the air is laced with skylark trill and curlew-speak.

Set off from the car park and turn right, walking along the main street (the A6), as far as a turning on the left at the fire station.

Shap is a place of some antiquity, having been granted a market charter in 1687; the odd-shaped market hall with curious windows and round arches stands on the main road, near the start of the walk; much of the stone for its building came from nearby Shap abbey following the Dissolution of the Monasteries. With motorway traffic thundering along not that far distant, it is difficult to believe now that this was the main thoroughfare between north and south, and that in winter it was often impassable.

The area around Shap has been inhabited since prehistoric times as standing stones and remains of stone circles testify. To the south of the village, **Shap Wells Hotel** was built in the 1830s to replace a small and somewhat indifferent inn that served the needs of visitors coming to 'take the waters' at Shap spa. Although never on

a par with Bath or Buxton, Shap Wells had its share of fame and attracted numerous members of the aristocracy. During the Second World War, the hotel was used as a prisoner of war camp for senior Luftwaffe and naval officers.

Turn left at the fire station and left again at Wells Close, then crossing to a footpath signpost directing you up an enclosed area at the rear of houses. This gives into a sloping, limestone-walled field at the top of which High Street,

Shap Abbey

Keld chapel

Kidsty Pike and the high fells on either side come into view. Head downfield now to a gap stile in a corner that feeds you into another, this time narrow, walled path, issuing then into a field in the middle of which stands a huge stone.

The Goggleby Stone is part of what little remains of an avenue of standing stones from Kemp Howe Stone Circle to the south (largely destroyed by the West Coast Mainline Railway), to a barrow farther north. Most of this avenue was destroyed at the time of the enclosure of common land (1760–1820), but a few remain. The Goggleby Stone is one such; another is the Thunder Stone (NY 551 157).

Keep forward alongside a wall, and on the far side of the field you intercept an old, walled track. Cross this and continue on a grassy path across two more fields. The path leads to a stile giving onto the narrow lane down to Keld, but it is possible to stay within the field boundary for a little while longer, although the stile exiting the field at the edge of Keld is rather more awkward to negotiate; better to leave the field at the earlier opportunity, and walk down the lane. As you enter Keld, you encounter its medieval chapel, a squat, rectangular structure shoe-horned into a wedge of

ground, and thought to date from the 15th century, when it was probably a chantry attached to Shap Abbey. This lovely, stone-built structure is now in the ownership of the National Trust, its interior of the most simple and rustic kind.

Press on through the village and out along a continuing lane leading onto the moorland beyond. Soon, you cross the River Lowther. Stay on the surfaced lane as you approach another bridge, with Shap Abbey tucked into the folds of the landscape off to your right. Even farther distant, you can pick out the undulating summits of the high Pennines, culminating in Cross Fell.

Eventually, you intercept another track **Ⓐ**, a concrete service road. Here turn right for Rayside. The road ultimately leads over the moors to Mardale, and sweeps on across tussocky, reedy moorland. The sense of openness and freedom is superb.

At the next junction **Ⓑ**, turn right down a rough-surfaced track towards Rayside. Follow the lane as far as a wall on the right **Ⓒ**. Here, leave the lane for a boggy path across rough pasture leading to a gate at a wall corner. Cross a stile, and go forward alongside a wall, and after about 100 yds, turn a wall corner, climbing a little, but then letting the wall guide you down through a dip and on to a ladder-stile in a field corner.

Having crossed the ladder-stile you find the River Lowther once more, and can cross a sloping pasture towards Shap Abbey. The path guides you to a steep bank overlooking a loop in the river. A path does descend the bank, but it is safer to stay above it and walk round to a stile, which avoids having to

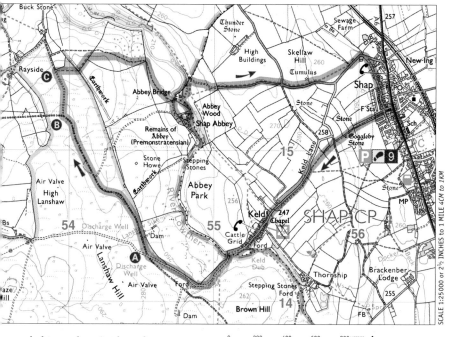

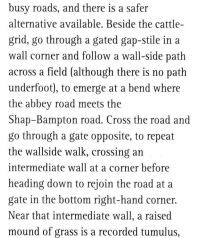

dodge overhanging branches.

Cross the stile, and go forward to visit the abbey. Shap Abbey, originally built at the very end of the 12th century, was among the last to be closed by Henry VIII. It belonged to an order founded by the German saint, Norbert, and owes its foundation to a baron named Thomas son of Gospatric. Very little is known about the history of the abbey. The order was of Premonstratensian monks and intended for those who wished to combine the life of prayer and discipline with parish work as priests serving local communities. Such men were known as White Canons from the colour of the habits they wore.

The end for Shap came on 14 January 1540, when the last abbot surrendered the abbey's possessions to the representatives of the Crown.

On leaving, cross the river by either of two bridges, and then follow a surfaced access lane that climbs across sloping pasture to a cattle-grid. You can now simply follow the walled lanes back to Shap, but these are seasonally busy roads, and there is a safer alternative available. Beside the cattle-grid, go through a gated gap-stile in a wall corner and follow a wall-side path across a field (although there is no path underfoot), to emerge at a bend where the abbey road meets the Shap–Bampton road. Cross the road and go through a gate opposite, to repeat the wallside walk, crossing an intermediate wall at a corner before heading down to rejoin the road at a gate in the bottom right-hand corner. Near that intermediate wall, a raised mound of grass is a recorded tumulus, possibly Bronze Age.

Turn left along the road towards Shap, but as it bends to the right, leave it for a lovely walled path on the right. This leads you behind houses and on to reach an estate road opposite West Close, where you began the walk. Now turn left to the main road, and then right to return to the car park. ●

Little Mell Fell

		GPS waypoints
Start	Thackthwaite	🖉 NY 417 252
Distance	4¼ miles (6.75km)	Ⓐ NY 414 241
Height gain	1,065 feet (325m)	Ⓑ NY 416 246
Approximate time	2½ hours	Ⓒ NY 429 238
Parking	Limited roadside parking along minor road	
Route terrain	Country lanes; open, grassy fellside	
Ordnance Survey maps	Landranger 90 (Penrith & Keswick), Explorer OL5 (The English Lakes – North-eastern area)	

The difficulties of finding somewhere safe and convenient to park should deter no one from tackling this exquisite little walk. With its slightly higher neighbour, Great Mell Fell (Walk 3), Little Mell Fell sits placidly to the south of the A66. This is uncomplicated walking – enjoyable, breathtaking and refreshing.

🖉 The lane that runs to the south of Thackthwaite does provide a few roadside indentations in which to park, and from wherever that might be, set off in a westerly direction. Wood sorrel in the hedgerows tells of a time when all of this area was wooded. Today it is open and offers lovely views northwards to Carrock Fell and Souther Fell, and ahead to Great Mell Fell. Determined walkers can link the two fells into one long day of the most agreeable fell wandering.

At a junction take the lane on the left, for Lowthwaite. Walking along this road is no hardship, sliding as it does across the western flank of Little Mell Fell high above the infant Dacre Beck, and with distant views of the Dodds and Helvellyn.

Go past the turning for Greenrow and Fox Hill, and finally leave the road, high above Foxhill Farm, for a vehicle track Ⓐ going up to a gate. Beyond the gate the track climbs a little farther but then swings back on itself, climbing

steadily through a rash of gorse. Cross a fence by a stile, and maintain the same direction passing through more gorse, and following a narrow path. Just as the path starts to descend you can branch right (NY 415 244), continuing to climb through gorse.

Once beyond the gorse, the ascending path broadens into an easy-angled rake, and rises to meet an old field boundary marked by a line of gnarled and twisted hawthorn Ⓑ. Cross the old boundary and climb the slope above, a brief, steep and pathless climb at the top of which the summit of Little Mell Fell hoves into view.

Now turn to head roughly in a southerly direction, up gently rising ground with the faintest suggestion of a path etched into the short, springy turf and moss. Once a fenceline comes into view ahead, backed by the ragged profile of Gowbarrow Fell set against that of Place Fell, bear left, turning now more in the direction of the summit.

As you approach the fence, go left

with it, and this will guide you to a fence corner where you can step over a fence from which barbs have been removed to enable you to do so. From the corner, head across an upland pasture towards a gate in another fence.

Once beyond the gate, simply follow a grassy path up on to the top of the fell, which is marked by a trig pillar. The geology of Little and Great Mell Fells is interesting as Carboniferous rocks form a conglomerate in which pebbles are set in a sandy matrix. Unusually the pebbles come from Skiddaw slate, Borrowdale Volcanic rocks, Coniston limestone, Silurian grit and even Shap granite. The assumption is that in the distant past they were carried to the Mell Fell site by powerful floods and resistant to erosion they now form the smooth, rounded fells visible today.

The popular line of ascent comes up from the south, but this walk continues across the summit in an easterly direction, towards what little you can just see of Ullswater. Before long the descent steepens as it heads down towards Mellfell House caravan park. After a while, the descending path peters out and you are left to determine your own way down.

As you descend, once you can locate an isolated house at the foot of the fell, this helps because now you can head towards it, and along the way you will intercept a lateral path. You have the choice of continuing the direct descent, but it is easier to turn left along the

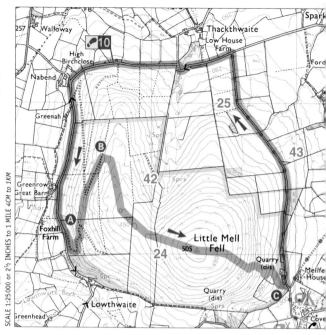

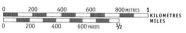

lateral path, descending gently until you can drop down to the right to a fence corner, next to a stream running down a gully.

Turn right, away from the fence corner, and follow the stream. When you reach a fence, where the stream changes direction, turn left. Had you made the direct descent, this is the point you would have been aiming for. Walk down beside a fence to a gate, and then by gates descend to meet a surfaced lane **C**.

On reaching the lane, turn immediately left – it's the first of two lanes on the left, climbing gently and proving to be a splendid track streaking northwards, a delight to follow with far-reaching views eastwards to Cross Fell, and north to Carrock Fell and Bowscale.

Eventually, the track descends to intercept the Thackthwaite road. Here, turn left and follow the road back to your starting point. ●

High Rigg and St John's in the Vale

		GPS waypoints
Start	Legburthwaite	📍 NY 318 195
Distance	5 miles (8km)	Ⓐ NY 311 209
Height gain	1,215 feet (370m)	Ⓑ NY 306 225
Approximate time	2½ hours	Ⓒ NY 314 213
Parking	Legburthwaite (Pay and Display)	
Route terrain	Undulating fell ridge; rock outcrops and grass; farmland; riverside path	
Ordnance Survey maps	Landranger 90 (Penrith & Keswick), Explorer OL5 (The English Lakes – North-eastern area)	

High Rigg (and the more northerly Low Rigg, visited in Walk 8) is a wedge of upland sandwiched between the bulk of High Seat and Castlerigg Fell to the west, and the Dodds beyond St John's Beck to the east. As a walking ground it is quite splendid, and largely ignored. The real beauty is that its many undulations and rocky outcrops are a canvas on which numerous ways can be drawn, the simplest being to follow the high ground. This walk describes such a high-level route, but you can virtually explore indiscriminately and find many sheltered nooks in which to wile away the hours contemplating the northern horizon of Skiddaw and Blencathra, or the crags of Clough Head to the east. Turn round and you can follow a route all the way up onto Helvellyn.

📍 The United Utilities car park at Legburthwaite is a perfect starting point, and from it you leave by a narrow gate giving onto an old, now gated, road. Turn left and walk out to the A591; there turn right, crossing a road bridge over St John's Beck, and shortly leaving the road at a gate and stile giving into the southern edge of the High Rigg domain.

A clear path now starts the ascent onto High Rigg. Shortly, when the path divides, branch left and simply follow its upward course, climbing steeply, among Scots pine. The steepness is relatively short-lived and the top of the first main rise is a good place to take in the surroundings, among which the craggy bulk of Castle Rock of Triermain is most prominent, protruding from the lower slopes of Watson's Dodd.

Castle Rock, long popular with rock gymnasts, was described by Walter Scott as the setting for his poem *The Bridal of Triermain*, in which he tells how the knight, Sir Roland, besieges the enchanted castle in search of the daughter of King Arthur and the Fairy Queen. He wrote: '... midmost of the vale, a mound Arose which airy turrets

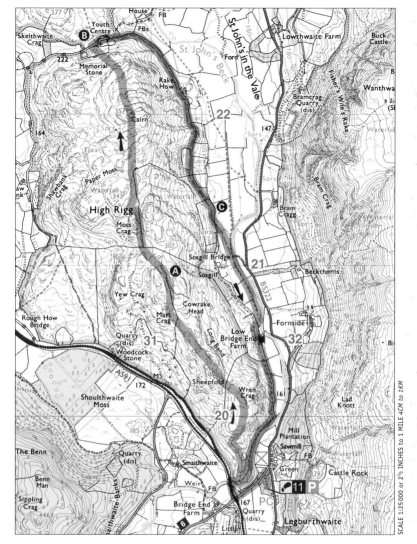

SCALE 1:25 000 or 2½ INCHES to 1 MILE 4CM to 1KM

crown'd, Buttress, and rampire's circling
bound, And mighty keep and tower;
Seem'd some primeval giant's hand, The
castle's massive walls had plann'd, A
ponderous bulwark ...'

The main path is never in doubt, and
slips down to pass through a wall gap,
beyond which a little scrambly shoulder
takes you to a fine viewpoint north
along the bumpy ridge – exactly what
the word 'rigg' means. And as you pass
through the long and delightful
succession of dips so you can watch the
mountains rise again and again; or turn

about to gaze upon Helvellyn, its lower
flanks now cleared of over-bearing
roadside trees. Thirlmere fills the dale,
flanked to the west by cloaks of pine
above which majestic Raven Crag puts
on a defiant show. It is all very inspiring
and, now that the ridge has been
gained, walking of the finest kind.

*When the path intercepts a fence at a
step-stile, you have the choice of
sticking to the main path, which will*

Looking north along High Rigg

lead you around and onward to meet a ladder-stile at a wall junction; or cross the stile and immediately turn right to walk beside a fence, past a small tarn **Ⓐ**. It is worth walking up onto the knoll above the tarn, for then the tarn features in a lovely picture of Clough Head; to do this, leave the fence-side path just as it levels, and branch left onto marginally higher ground, from which there are numerous ways of returning to the tarn. Un-named, but not unreasonably High Rigg Tarn, this small lake ringed by bogbean and rushes, is the only one of High Rigg's many small tarns that does not dry up seasonally.

Beyond the tarn, you gradually descend to a wall junction, where the regular path re-appears. Cross a ladder-stile here, and walk up beside a wall. The path moves away to pass around the end of a small, boggy area. Again there is the choice of doubling back towards the wall, or of heading onto higher ground.

As the wall changes direction, simply keep forward to reach the top of High Rigg, a perfect crown, topped by a cairn of modest girth. From the summit a path tumbles northwards to the church of St John's in the Vale **Ⓑ**, lying, almost unseen from above, along the narrow road that here crosses the fell, and that was once a main thoroughfare linking the dales on either side. Beyond this hiatus, the ridge continues northwards to blue-eyed Tewet Tarn, but for the present walk, once reaching the church-side road, turn right, and descend a short distance until, just after the end of the graveyard, you can leave the road at a gate and stile for a broad track, a bridleway, that now provides a simple, mildly undulating, and very therapeutic scamper southwards, high above St John's Beck.

The onward route is straightforward, and leads to Low Bridge End Farm. As you head towards the farm you first encounter a swathe of woodland. Before reaching it, keep an eye open for a single arch bridge that seems to be floating in the middle of a pasture on your left. A gate **Ⓒ** gives access to the pasture and an indistinct path leads towards the bridge (Sosgill Bridge). Just on reaching the bridge, and without crossing it, turn right onto the top of a flood embankment that leads on beside St John's Beck to the edge of Low Bridge End Farm.

Pass a large open barn, and then bear right on a path that takes you round the edge of the farm, which, for those in need of refreshment, will be found to have a small **tea garden**. Beyond the farm the path drops to become a broad path alongside a wall, there is every likelihood that this is an old Church Path. Castle Rock looms ahead, as the path climbs above the beck before running out to meet the A591 again, rejoining the outward route. Turn left and shortly left again along the old road to return to the car park. ●

Glenridding and Lanty's Tarn

		GPS waypoints	
Start	Glenridding		
Distance	5¼ miles (8.3km)	✐ NY 386 169	
Height gain	1,015 feet (310m)	Ⓐ NY 379 169	
		Ⓑ NY 363 173	
Approximate time	2½ hours	Ⓒ NY 376 167	
Parking	Glenridding (Pay and Display)	Ⓓ NY 381 159	
Route terrain	Stony tracks; some road walking; open fellside		
Ordnance Survey maps	Landranger 90 (Penrith & Keswick), Explorer OL5 (The English Lakes – North-eastern area)		

The renown of Glenridding as one of the key tourist hotspots of the Lake District is far reaching. From here walkers launch themselves into the hills, while less energetic moments can be spent along the lakeshore or taking to one of the steamers that regularly ply up and down the lake. This was once a major mining area, and a veritable hive of industrial activity in years gone by. Taking the opportunity to visit the mining area, this walk then slips southwards into neighbouring Grisedale by way of secluded Lanty's Tarn, a spot quiet enough to attract goosander at some times of year.

✐ Leave the main car park by walking out to the road and turning right to cross Glenridding Bridge, and then immediately right onto a narrow lane for Miresbeck and Helvellyn. Walk past a whitewashed cottage with circular chimneys typical of the Lake District, and probably dating from the late 18th century. Beyond this the lane becomes a stony track. When it forks, branch right and go towards Glenridding Beck, now following a lovely track around a camp site to emerge onto a surfaced lane at Gillside.

Turn right and cross Rattlebeck Bridge Ⓐ. The on-going lane comes out at a wider road. Go left, climbing gently and when, shortly, it forks, keep left

again for Greenside Mine and Sticks Pass, to pass below rows of terraced cottages that once served the miners and their families.

The fells on your right (north) are Glenridding Dodd and Sheffield Pike *(see Walk 14)*, while to the south looms the massive bulk of Birkhouse Moor. The ongoing track is most agreeable and ambles up towards the main mining site. Lead ore was first discovered at what became the Greenside Lead Mine in the 1650s, the first levels being driven by Dutch adventurers in the 1690s, and dressed ore was carried to the Stoneycroft smelter at Keswick. Production at the mine, however, did not really begin until the late 18th

Eagle Cottage, Glenridding

hostel and mountain huts; in fact, a bridge seat at Swart Beck is a perfect place to take a breather.

Follow the path as it ascends past the youth hostel, crosses Swart Beck and then by a waymarked route threads a group of buildings to take a waymarked track for Red Tarn and Helvellyn. The path climbs to a footbridge **B** spanning the upper reaches of Glenridding Beck, here flowing down from Keppel Cove.

Over the bridge turn left and take to the course of an old leat, which cuts an almost level path across the slopes of Birkhouse Moor. Another option takes a lower course, running along a woodland boundary and then a wall.

century, and the mine was not extensively worked until 1825, when mining activity reached its height following the setting up of the Greenside Mining Company in 1822. Power was originally provided by waterwheels, with the water being supplied by the damming of nearby tarns. One of them, Keppel Cove, burst its banks on October 29, 1927, bringing disaster to the village below. Much the same happened four years later, when flood waters smashed through the concrete of High Dam.

At the height of its activity, the Greenside Mine was not only the largest lead mine in the Lake District, with over 300 employees, but was also a pioneer, being the first to use electricity to power the winding gear, and it also ran the first underground electric engine in British ore mines.

By the early 1960s it had become uneconomic to continue to extract lead from the mine, and it closed, the last ore being extracted in April 1961. But that was not entirely the end of the story for the mine was then used to test instruments designed to detect underground nuclear explosions. Most of the mine buildings are now gone, but a few remain and see service as a youth

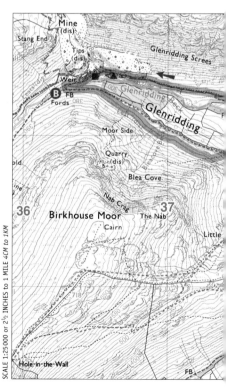

SCALE 1:25000 or 2½ INCHES to 1 MILE 4CM to 1KM

But the leat is of admirable purpose, and much preferred, finally concluding at a low wall that deflects walkers down to the lower path.

Now walk beside a wall to a ladder-stile and gate **C**, where you pass onto a descending stony track that comes down to intercept a rough track serving a nearby cottage. Bear right and cross a footbridge, now taking to a path for Grisedale and Lanty's Tarn. Pass through a wall gap and then pursue a waymarked route across rough pasture.

The path leads up to a gate in a wall from which it continues, climbing easily through another gate and generally towards a shroud of trees that surround Lanty's Tarn. As you crest a rise, Lanty's Tarn comes into view, just beyond a gate. Pass to the right of the tarn, emerging on the other side to a splendid view of Grisedale. Quite who 'Lanty' of Lanty's Tarn was, is unknown; perhaps a smuggler or illicit whisky distiller, both activities being prevalent across the Lake District in the past. The tarn is formed by a low dam, and the probability is that this was done by the Marshalls at Patterdale Hall; reputedly there is an underground cellar below the dam which may well have been used as an ice house, such not being uncommon, although there is no conclusive evidence of this.

As you pass the far end of the tarn, the path drops towards Grisedale, and affords ever-improving views up this delightful valley *(see Walk 18)*. Eventually you approach a couple of gates, both of which give on to the track up to Striding Edge *(Walk 22)*. Take the left-hand gate **D** and then turn left down a sloping pasture to a gate at the bottom giving on to a narrow lane. Follow this across Grisedale Beck and out to a T-junction, there turning left to follow a surfaced lane down past Patterdale Hall and out to meet the main valley road.

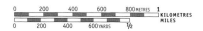

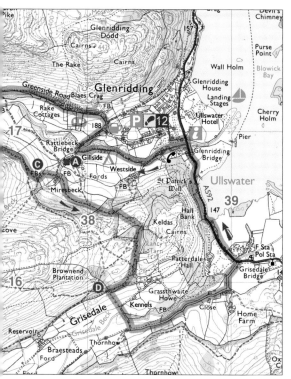

The hall, not open to the public, is substantially rebuilt, but dates from around 1677.

Turn left at the road and cross to a path opposite, soon branching onto a path through roadside trees. A short way farther on you pop out onto the road again. Cross with care and continue onto a raised footpath on the opposite side, later re-crossing the road for the final stretch back into the centre of Glenridding.

Adam Seat and Harter Fell

		GPS waypoints
Start	Mardale Head	NY 469 107
Distance	4½ miles (7km)	Ⓐ NY 474 092
Height gain	1,755 feet (535m)	Ⓑ NY 459 093
Approximate time	2½ hours	Ⓒ NY 452 096
Parking	Mardale Head	
Route terrain	Rough, stony fell tracks and summits; steep descent	
Ordnance Survey maps	Landranger 90 (Penrith & Keswick), Explorer OL5 (The English Lakes – North-eastern area)	

Mardale is a beautiful retreat, flanked by fine fells, and, if you want to be maudlin, with a sad story to tell. The people who settled here and remained until the 1930s, in spite of their undoubted hardships, must have known they were living somewhere special. And it is heartening to think that from time to time those long-dead shepherds might have wandered up onto the fells and gazed down on their valley home with just a smattering of contentment. There is no finer place for taking in the whole dale than the top of Harter Fell. This walk shares a start with Walk 17, up to the Gatescarth Pass, but then heads in the opposite direction for a short but energetic circuit at the head of the dale.

Set off through the gate at Mardale Head and take the path rising on the left, a stony trod that climbs steadily, zigzagging when to do so eases the gradient, all the way to the fence and gate at the top of Gatescarth Pass Ⓐ. This is an ancient thoroughfare, and

Mardale Head

would have seen regular use by packhorse trains in the 18th and 19th centuries.

Just before reaching the top of the pass, a broad track sweeps upwards on the right. This relatively new trail leads directly to Harter Fell, passing first over the craggy upthrust of Little Harter Fell. But, instead of taking this popular way, climb in a south-westerly direction alongside the fence following a grassy path to the summit of Adam Seat. Here the view opens up southwards down the great valley of Longsleddale and across the Shap Fells to Tarn Crag and Gray Crag, and towards hidden Crookdale.

The summit of Adam Seat is marked by a fine steeple-like marker bearing the letters 'L', on one side and 'H' on the

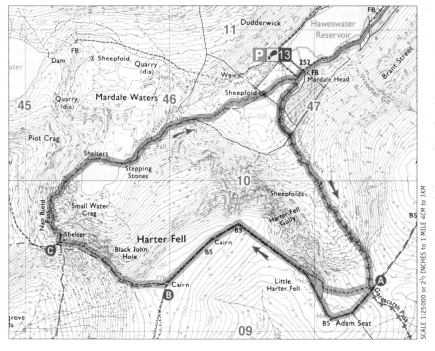

side facing Kendal. The first is clearly for Lowther, the second letter's significance however is not clear, perhaps the Howards of Greystoke.

Press on beside the fence and eventually join a broad stony track that leads up to the summit of Harter Fell **B**. On the way, and just after the fenceline

Harter Fell

changes direction, a cairn marks the finest view of Mardale.

From the top of Harter Fell, you set off in a westerly direction, descending steeply on a clear path through rocky terrain until you reach the Nan Bield Pass **C**, where there is a small shelter. Like Gatescarth, this, too, is an ancient packhorse trail crossing point.

At the pass, you now turn northwards and descend around Small Water, following a clear and mainly stony path back down to Mardale Head. ●

Sheffield Pike and Glenridding Dodd

		GPS waypoints	
Start	Glencoynedale foot		
Distance	5 miles (8km)	✎	NY 386 189
Height gain	1,935 feet (590m)	Ⓐ	NY 375 184
		Ⓑ	NY 362 182
Approximate time	3 hours	Ⓒ	NY 373 178
Parking	At start (Pay and Display)	Ⓓ	NY 378 175
Route terrain	Rough fell walking; steep descent; a little road walking		
Ordnance Survey maps	Landranger 90 (Penrith & Keswick), Explorer OL5 (The English Lakes – North-eastern area)		

Sheffield Pike suffers from the proximity of higher fare in the shape of Helvellyn, which tends to cloud the minds of the masses bound for the fells. But discerning fell explorers are always to be found pottering about on Sheffield Pike whether having ascended from Glenridding, or, as here, via lovely Glencoynedale. Adding Glenridding Dodd to the day's tally will tax no one, and reward with arguably the finest view there is of the southern end of Ullswater.

✎ A large car park just north of Glencoynedale is a near perfect place to begin, except for the incidence of about 200 yds dodging the Formula 1 mayhem of a busy road without a verge; care is needed as you turn right out of the car park and head south to the entrance to Glencoyne Farm. Thankfully this is short-lived and soon you can turn right towards the farm.

On the way you cross Glencoyne Bridge, nice enough in itself, but especially significant to those who love the landscapes of the now defunct county of Westmorland, for Glencoyne Beck marks the boundary between the county and what was Cumberland.

As you approach Glencoyne Farm you cannot help but notice the distinctive, large, round chimneys that

are so characteristic of the vernacular architecture of the 18th century, the farm being constructed in 1787. The farm was probably under the management of a yeoman farmer, one of that small, independent owner-occupier of farms that were a distinguishing feature of Cumbrian rural society. This secluded dwelling, is perhaps better seen across the pastures at the end of the walk, when it appears perfectly placed against the fells of Hart Side and Watermillock Common. John Robinson's *Guide to the Lakes* published in 1819, describes the farm '... embowered in trees, and standing under a range of rocks, which command a fine view of the middle bend of the lake.'

On reaching the farm, bear to the right, and go past the farmhouse and then turn left between the farmhouse and a byre (or go a little farther and turn left after the byre in order to be a little less intrusive) to gain a path, not immediately obvious, but climbing steeply and becoming a clear grooved track across a sloping pasture.

Continue with the path, now amply clear, to pass below the cottages at Seldom Seen. The cottages, originally built for miners, now see service as holiday lets, and it is perhaps whimsical to imagine that the name refers to the out-of-the-way nature of this comely dale, which just gets better the higher you go.

The path presses on, as if going all the way into Glencoynedale, but at a low waymark, you bear left, ascending on a grassy path towards a wall and then running below it until you reach a gate **A** at a wall corner. Through the

gate, turn right beside a wall, and follow this as it ascends steadily to a wall corner, with the great bowl of Glencoyne Head rising beyond to soft-moulded Green Side and Hart Side.

After a brief pull up from the gate, a splendid terrace path now follows for a while, until it starts to climb again as it crosses Bleabank Side and rises to a neat col at Nick Head **B**. Just as you approach Nick Head, the path divides. Branch left, taking the higher path with improving views across the intervening gulf of Glenridding to pyramidal Catstye Cam set against the dark cliffs of Helvellyn and the knobbly ridge of Striding Edge.

Just above Nick Head a metal boundary pole bears the date 1912 and the initials 'H' and 'M'; it marks the boundary of land between Howard of Greystoke and Marshall of Patterdale Hall; a similar pole will be found later on, near the top of Heron Pike. A peaty path now leads up to the top of

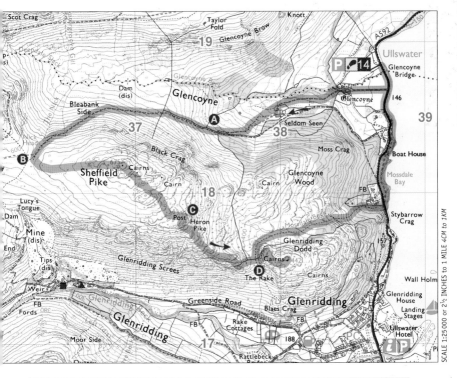

Place Fell from Glenridding Dodd

Sheffield Pike, crowned by a fine cairn.

The continuation from Sheffield Pike summit needs a little care to begin with, just to ensure you locate the correct path, first to Heron Pike and then onwards and downwards. The main direction is south-east, and a clear and continuous path takes you first to Heron Pike **C**, from where you need to look to the southern side of the fell to locate another narrow path, tortuous and twisting in delightful fashion that guides you down to a wall gap just above the col linking to Glenridding Dodd **D**.

The ascent of Glenridding Dodd is straightforward, setting off alongside a wall, but then abandoning the wall and curving back to the right to climb onto the top of the fell. The first large cairn you reach is the summit, but there are more cairns farther to the east, and the last of these marks a stupendous viewpoint that more than amply rewards the little extra effort.

Return to the col, and a gate through the wall, beyond which, a grassy trod sets off into Mossdale. The path soon joins Mossdale Beck, a delightful companion, with fine retrospective views of Heron Pike. Lower down, the path enters a spread of larch trees where a little ducking, diving and limbo dancing is needed to make progress. The path is continuous, but is not well used, and so it appears uncertain in places.

Eventually, the path descends to meet a fence. Turn left alongside this to a low step-stile nearby, over which you continue the descent to the valley road (A592); the last 100 yds of the descent are messy and slippery.

Cross the road and turn left, soon stepping off the road and onto a fine permissive path around the edge of Mossdale Bay that runs parallel with, but protected from, the busy road. It is a fine end to a fine walk, offering delightful cameos of the lake and its Norfolk Island through the trees. In the end, the path is forced back onto the road, leaving you with about 440 yds of careful walking to return to the car park. On the way, if traffic permits, take a moment or two to look at Glencoyne Farm across the roadside pasture. ●

Beda Fell

		GPS waypoints	
Start	Martindale	🖉	NY 433 190
Distance	5½ miles (9km)	**Ⓐ**	NY 432 183
Height gain	1,510 feet (460m)	**Ⓑ**	NY 430 186
Approximate time	3 hours	**Ⓒ**	NY 418 158
Parking	Martindale, limited at Howegrain Beck bridge	**Ⓓ**	NY 433 165
Route terrain	Open fell ridge; numerous rocky outcrops; some road walking		
Ordnance Survey maps	Landranger 90 (Penrith & Keswick), Explorer OL5 (The English Lakes – North-eastern area)		

Separating the valleys of Boredale and Bannerdale at the bottom end of the long cul-de-sac that runs down the eastern shores of Ullswater from Pooley Bridge, Beda Fell will prove a most delightful surprise. This knobbly ridge offers an outstanding line of ascent that leads ultimately to the Angletarn Pikes, but crams a huge amount of walking pleasure into its circuit, leaving you with a distinct appetite for more.

🖉 The walk begins from the bridge spanning Howegrain Beck at Martindale, although there is more parking near the church on the hause to the north-east; this would add little to the overall distance, but means a short, sharp uphill finish.

Cross the bridge, following the road for around 150 yds to locate a broad track doubling back on the left. Turn up this, although you will find that it can be reached just as easily by a steep path from just after the bridge. Follow the track past a cottage, beyond which it continues parallel with a wall to rejoin the road at Winter Crag, a white-painted cottage **Ⓐ**. Do not quite reach the road, but instead, turn right at a slate waymark onto a rising grassy path in a north-westerly direction.

For a while, the path and a wall climb together, but then part company as the wall descends to the right and the path

climbs to a low col at the northern end of Beda Fell. A convenient bench **Ⓑ**, with a fine view over Boredale and Ullswater to Gowbarrow Fell, is an excellent place to regain your breath.

Now turn left to climb southwards

The summit of Beda Fell

along the ridge, the path rising repeatedly in simple steps as it tackles persistent rocky upthrusts. Higher up the ridge, the path divides, but it matters not which route you choose, as both rejoin later. That on the left is at an easier gradient, and is therefore a little longer.

Once the paths are reunited, the route continues along the crest of the ridge, now with the Beda Head, the summit of the ridge, in view.

The highest point of the fell is topped by two small cairns. Continue across the summit on a grassy path, and, after a few low grassy bumps, you begin a beautiful gradual descent towards Bedafell Knott, the final rock outcrop of the ridge before it links with Angletarn Pikes.

The top of Bedafell Knott is marked by a small cairn. Press on beyond it, but only for a short distance farther until you reach a cross-path **⊙**, where there is also a cairn.

(Strong walkers may want to scamper further along the ridge to visit Angletarn Pikes, and then return to this crossing point, an ancient bridleway

Pikeawassa from Beda Fell

that would have seen considerable use in years gone by as one of the principal thoroughfares across the valleys of Martindale Common.)

At the cross-path, turn abruptly left (north-east), to begin what will prove a delightful descent high above Bannerdale to the farm at Dale Head.

Across the valley, on the lower slopes of Wether Hill you can see a red-roofed building; this is The Bungalow, a hunting lodge built by the fifth Earl of Lonsdale, Hugh Cecil Lowther. The earl was a passionate sportsman and bon vivant, and known as 'England's greatest sporting gentleman'; he donated the original Lonsdale Belts for boxing.

Lord Lonsdale was also the inspiration for the Lonsdale cigar size, and was part of a famous wager with John Pierpoint Morgan over whether a man could circumnavigate the globe and remain unidentified.

He was known as the 'Yellow Earl' for his penchant for the colour. He was a founder and first president of the Automobile Association (AA) which adopted his livery.

The track comes down to a gate, from which it drops to run alongside a wall

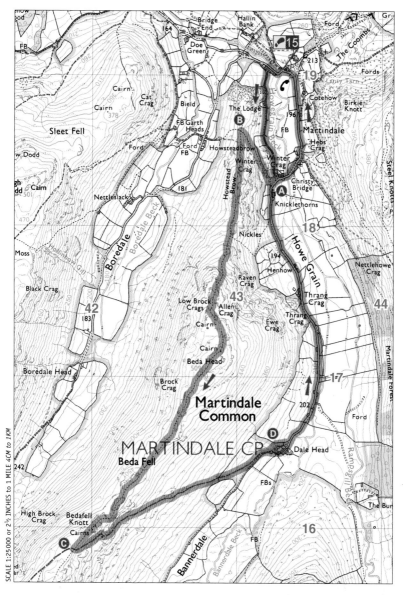

heading for Dale Head Farm **D** .

As you reach the farm there are two possible ways. One is to go through a gate on the right and walk through the farmyard; the other stays above the gate and follows a permissive route above the farm buildings and across a stream to locate a narrow gate. Both routes rejoin at the road head, and now all that remains is to follow this quiet farm lane back to the white-painted building at Winter Crag **A**.

Here you have the choice of returning along the bridleway used at the start of the walk, or of remaining on the road to pass the nearby church and follow the road. At a road junction, you descend left to return to the bridge over Howegrain Beck and complete the walk. ●

Pooley Bridge and Barton Park

Pooley Bridge
and Barton Park

		GPS waypoints
Start	Pooley Bridge	
Distance	6 miles (9.5km)	NY 469 245
Height gain	770 feet (235m)	Ⓐ NY 460 226
		Ⓑ NY 459 213
Approximate time	3 hours	Ⓒ NY 482 222
Parking	Pooley Bridge (Pay and Display)	Ⓓ NY479 236
Route terrain	Lakeshore; farmland; open fell	
Ordnance Survey maps	Landranger 90 (Penrith & Keswick), Explorer OL5 (The English Lakes – North-eastern area)	

The eastern side of Ullswater, accessible from Pooley Bridge has always been a delight; relative inaccessibility lends a note of intrigue and arouses curiosity, although today visitors come in increasing numbers by steamer from Glenridding. But anyone starting this walk mid-afternoon in summer will be rewarded with a tranquility and light that is deeply satisfying. The walk touches on High Street, the Roman road, and visits an area inhabited since prehistoric times, but there is much that is random about the route, and the scope for wandering off to explore a little more widely should not be ignored.

Begin from the Dunmallard car park at Pooley Bridge, close by the River Eamont. Cross the road bridge and on the other side turn right between gate pillars at the entrance to Eusemere Lodge.

Lined with old stone cottages and houses that exude a rustic charm, Pooley Bridge flanks the River Eamont, the former boundary between Cumberland and Westmorland. Before the bridge was built in the 16th century, the village was simply called Pooley, a corruption of 'pool by the hill'. The hill in this case is Dunmallet – or Dunmallard, as it is known these days – which bears a small and undistinguished Iron Age fort *(see Walk 1)*.

Eusemere, south-east of the village was the home of Catherine Clarkson, the wife of anti-slavery campaigner Thomas Clarkson (1760-1846). Mrs Clarkson, referred to as such throughout her journals, was a close friend of Dorothy Wordsworth, and both Clarksons and Wordsworths spent much time together and in correspondence.

Walk along a rough-surfaced lane for about 90 yds before turning right onto a signposted path for the lakeshore, leading to a gate. A broad track ensues, passing through another gate and then reaching the shores of Ullswater. Continue along the water's edge and pass a landing stage, always following the lakeshore to reach yet another gate.

The ongoing path is never far from the lakeshore and eventually reaches farm buildings and a camping park at

Waterside House. Go forward past farm buildings, but then at the entrance to the campsite turn left along a short access track to reach a narrow lane.

Turn right and follow the lane for about 550 yds, as far as the turning to Cross Dormont . Here leave the lane and turn up an access track, but just before reaching the farm buildings, bear right to a step-stile beside a gate. Go half-left to another stile, and then bear half-right to yet another and a waymark by the edge of a caravan site.

Cross the stile and continue beside a fence to a stile near the end of a low farm building. Over this, go forward onto a footpath for Howtown Road via Crook-a-dyke. Keep forward between walls to a gate, and there immediately bear left to a low step-stile, and then walk around a field edge. On the far side of the field, a through-stile beside a wooden gate gives onto a continuing

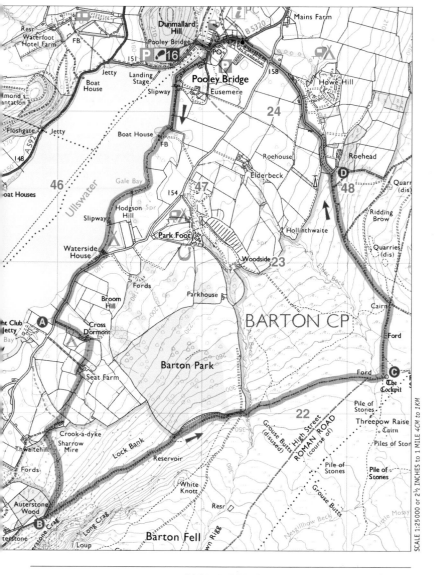

Ullswater, near Pooley Bridge

path beside a wall, which later swings left to pass alongside a narrow beck. Cross the stream to a gate and, in the ensuing field, maintain the same direction to the right-hand edge of a barn at Crook-a-dyke Farm. Now keep forward on a vehicle track for Howtown and Martindale.

As the track bears right towards Thwaitehill Farm, leave it by turning towards a gate in the intake wall, which gives onto a narrow track through rough pasture. The path leads through a broad spread of gorse, and then climbs easily towards Auterstone Wood. Keep following a clear, grassy path to reach the woodland, and press on a little further to intercept a broad track **B** rising to the left across the base of Barton Fell, which soars quite steeply above the route. Turn left onto the track, for Moor Divock and Helton.

The track climbs steadily and then levels as it approaches the top edge of more woodland, Barton Park. Continue on a clear path above the top edge of the woodland and keep following its boundary wall, which leads to a shallow ravine containing Aik Beck.

Immediately after crossing Aik Beck, take the lower of two paths and press on across open moorland, heading towards the low dome of Heughscar Hill. The track eventually crosses another at a cairn, which marks the interception with the Roman road, High Street, linking the forts at Ambleside and Brougham.

Keep forward beyond the cairn to reach the head of another stream, Elder Beck, just beyond which the track reaches the edge of a low stone circle, known as The Cockpit **C**. Little is known about The Cockpit. As a stone circle it is not especially impressive, although it is actually a concentric ring. The date is unknown, but probably Bronze Age like the numerous barrows and cairns dotted about the top of adjacent Askham Fell. The name suggests that the site may well have been used in the past as an arena for fighting cocks, but it is unlikely that it would have been built for this purpose.

From The Cockpit, follow the track as it bears left (ignore the track across the moor). This leads on to intercept another track at a large cairn, just below Heughscar Hill, having followed the Roman road for a short distance. But at the cairn, leave this ancient highway by turning left onto a very broad service track that descends easily above the northern reaches of Ullswater to reach the top end of a surfaced lane at Roehead **D**.

Now simply follow the lane downwards to return to Pooley Bridge. At the crossroads, keep forward into the village and eventually reach the bridge once more, turning right to return to the car park. ●

Branstree and Selside Pike

		GPS waypoints
Start	Mardale Head	

Distance	5½ miles (9.2km)
Height gain	1,740 feet (530m)
Approximate time	3 hours
Parking	Mardale Head
Route terrain	Moorland fell tops with few distinguishing features
Ordnance Survey maps	Landranger 90 (Penrith & Keswick), Explorer OL5 (The English Lakes – North-eastern area)

GPS waypoints

- ✎ NY 469 107
- Ⓐ NY 474 092
- Ⓑ NY 494 123

Most walkers visiting the roadhead at Mardale are bound for the summits around High Street (see Walk 19), or visiting to see if they can spot any remains of the village of Mardale, drowned with the raising of the reservoir in the 1930s, taking with it a way of life so poignantly exemplified by Sarah Hall in her novel Haweswater.

But the heights to the east of the roadhead, those of Mardale Common and Swindale Common, are a real reward for anyone wanting solitude and quiet days. This and Walk 13 share a common start, but then head in opposite directions to explore less well-known summits, nevertheless well worthy of investigation.

From Mardale the slopes of Branstree, the first summit, are suitable only for walkers with calf muscles like barrage balloons and something to prove. Luckily for lesser mortals, like the author, there is a much more agreeable route.

✎ Leave the roadhead at Mardale and walk through a gate, taking the left-hand stony track that rises steadily, parallel with the boundary of a nearby plantation, but then changing direction below the craggy face of Harter Fell to fashion a splendid ascent never far from the company of Gatescarth Beck.

Gatescarth is the name of the pass to which you are ascending, and it is a walk of pure delight to amble upwards at a steady plod until you reach a gate

and fence across the pass Ⓐ. This was something of a trade route in the past linking two dales. Beyond the pass, the ground falls swiftly into the head of Long Sleddale. It is all remote and wonderful, a glorious mess of crags, becks, walls and mire.

For the moment, on reaching the pass, from where a clear path carrying *Walk 13* sets off in a westerly direction onto Harter Fell, simply pass through the gate and turn immediately left beside the fence. Dance around a small boggy patch of ground in a dip, and then engage an easy pull on grass, beside the fence, all the way to the top of Branstree. Cross the fence by a step-stile close by a wall.

The summit of Branstree is singularly

undistinguished, lying a short distance from the stile, and marked by a collapsed cairn of modest girth and a ground-level, circular triangulation station of a type rarely found in the Lake District.

From the summit, a clear grassy trod leads out to a couple of remarkable cairns on Artle Crag, to which you should press on. From the second cairn you easily reach a path beside the fence, and, by-passing an un-named summit off to the east and a survey pillar used during the construction of Haweswater, you simply follow the arrow-straight fenceline to the slight depression known as Captain Whelter Bog, a trap for the unwary only in very wet conditions. From here a clear path rises quickly onto the top of Selside Pike, marked by a large shelter-cairn.

On Selside Pike you quit the fenceline and launch into fell moorland without anything useful as a guide. But from the shelter two paths can be seen, one with a low metal post planted in it. Ignore this, and take the path on the left, slightly more pronounced, and good enough to guide you all the way down to intercept the Old Corpse Road west of Swindale Head **B**. The corpse road was used to convey the dead of Mardale on the backs of packhorses to the nearest churchyard for burial. The route crosses into Swindale and then traverses high moorland to Shap. The last such journey was made in 1736, by which time the right of burial had been granted to the tiny Holy Trinity church in Mardale Green, which recorded its

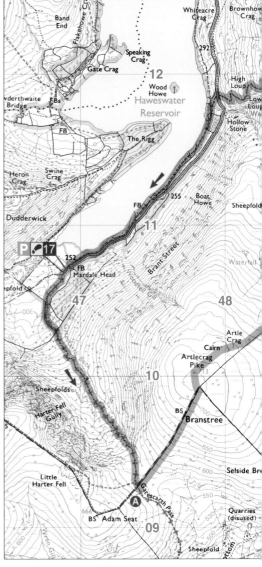

first burial in 1726. When, by 1936, plans to raise Haweswater and submerge Mardale Green were finalised, the burials made at Holy Trinity were disinterred and reburied at Shap. You intercept the corpse road at a wooden pole; here, turn left, and walk gently uphill to another pole on the skyline. This waymark is the high point

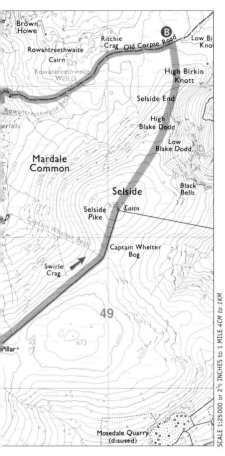

The summit of Branstree, with Selside Pike in the distance

The large cairn on Artle Crag

of the crossing, a spot that must have brought a moment's welcome respite to those in charge of conveying coffins across the moors, not least the packhorses.

The way is now all downhill, although there is nothing at all downhill about the quality of the landscape. For some distance the path potters about among numerous rocky outcrops and boggy dips, but then, with Haweswater and the fells to the west now fully in view, it begins its descent in earnest, dropping steeply to pass the ruins of a couple of buildings with the waterfalls of Rowantreethwaite Beck and Hopgill Beck appearing on the left.

The descending track eventually comes down to meet the valley road at a gate. Go left, crossing the road, to another gate opposite, from which a concessionary path runs back to Mardale Head at varying distances from the lakeshore. Its first task, however, is to cross the combined forces of Hopgill Beck and Rowantreethwaite Beck, which it does by means of a neat single-arch bridge. Beyond that, the path is clear enough and leads unerringly back to the start. ●

SCALE 1:25000 or 2½ INCHES to 1 MILE 4CM to 1KM

Grisedale

		GPS waypoints	
Start	Patterdale	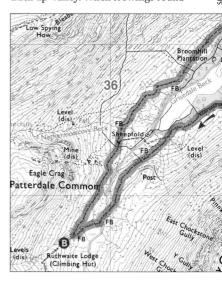 NY 396 159	
Distance	7 miles (11km)	**A** NY 382 156	
Height gain	1,280 feet (390m)	**B** NY 357 137	
Approximate time	3½ hours	**C** NY 381 159	
Parking	Opposite Patterdale Hotel (Pay and Display)	**D** NY 389 159	
Route terrain	Rough fell paths, often rocky but always clear		
Ordnance Survey maps	Landranger 90 (Penrith & Keswick), Explorer OL5 (The English Lakes – North-eastern area)		

Grisedale tends to lose out as a place to visit because most walkers are either heading up on to Striding Edge or St Sunday Crag. There is an exception – the walkers following the Northern Coast-to-Coast route, which slips down the valley from Grisedale Tarn. The reality is that this rugged dale, much given to farming and some rather striking drystone walls, is a gem and well worth wandering up and down at any time of the year.

Turn left out of the car park, cross the road and, opposite the **White Lion hotel**, turn right onto a path climbing past **public toilets**. At the rear of an isolated building, leave the track by turning left onto a path through bracken and heather, that leads to a gate.

The path climbs through rocks and small boulders for a short while before descending to a kissing-gate to the left of two other gates. Through this, follow the continuing wall, then climb to a horizontal path before descending gently to cross Hag Beck on stepping stones. The path runs on easily across the slopes of Glenamara Park and the steeper slopes below Thornhow End.

Follow the path as it leads alongside a wall bounding a pine plantation, and then maintain a level course as the wall drops away to the right. A short way on, the path rejoins a wall and arrives at a gate. Pass through this gate and

continue descending beside a wall to a couple of sheepfolds. There turn right through another wall gate, going down-field, past a barn to a surfaced track **A**.

Now simply turn left and follow the track up-valley. When it swings round

SCALE 1:25 000 or 2½ INCHES to 1 MILE 4CM to 1KM

to access Braesteads Farm, keep ahead onto a graded track to Elmhow Farm. After Elmhow Farm, the path becomes increasingly rugged as the route penetrates to the heart of the high fells into a harsher, mountain landscape. There is a keen sense of remoteness here, but a fine feeling as all around fellslopes (and walls) soar upwards.

Continue climbing, with increasing ruggedness underfoot until Grisedale Beck is crossed. A rough path leads on to join a path descending from nearby Ruthwaite Lodge. At this turning point, cross another footbridge **B** in order to begin the return journey. A splendid path now surges back down the valley, giving welcome views of waterfalls not seen on the ascent, and passing through the intake wall below Nethermostcove Beck.

Keep following the descending path, which re-ascends briefly after passing above Braesteads Farm. Eventually it arrives at a wall corner, where there are two gates **C**. Go through the right-hand one, and down-field to a surfaced farm access below.

Head down the access road to cross lively Grisedale Beck. At a T-junction, turn left and follow a surfaced lane until it makes a pronounced left turn. Here leave it by branching right onto a wide track **D**.

Shortly, leave the track at a waymark, pass through a kissing-gate, and follow a waymarked route across rough pasture to a high through-stile in a wall. Over the wall you rejoin the outward route. Turn left to follow it back to the start. ●

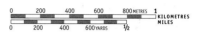

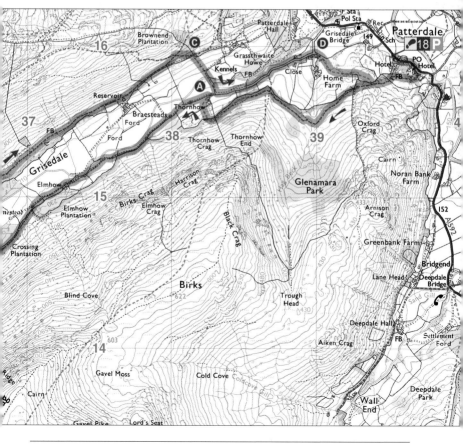

Rough Crag and High Street

		GPS waypoints
Start	Mardale Head	 NY 469 107
Distance	5½ miles (9km)	Ⓐ NY 473 114
Height gain	2,100 feet (640m)	Ⓑ NY 442 113
Approximate time	3½ hours	Ⓒ NY 452 096
Parking	Mardale Head	
Route terrain	Rough mountain walking; steep and long ascents and descents	
Ordnance Survey maps	Landranger 90 (Penrith & Keswick), Explorer OL5 (The English Lakes – North-eastern area)	

During the course of a year, many walkers visit the flat-topped summit of High Street; it has the attraction of elevation, good views and fits neatly into a number of entertaining circuits. But only discerning walkers take to the rocky approach offered by Rough Crag. Close scrutiny of the map reveals a more sensible line to the south, one that becomes an outstanding ridge walk.

The walk begins from the car park at the road end in Mardale. Parking is limited and free, so arrive early. The setting is magnificent, with high, rocky, steep-sided fells forming the valley head. Go through the nearby gate, and turn right beside a wall, to cross Mardale Beck, and right again, heading for the mature stand of larch and spruce that colonise The Rigg. As you approach the trees, the path starts rising, and finally meets the low end of a ridge at a gap in a wall Ⓐ.

Just before the wall, go left, over a small hillock cloaked in bracken, with the formidable end of Rough Crag towering above you. It seems impregnable, but a path threads a way through or round all obstacles on the way. The going is far less rough than the name suggests, but it remains steep, at least until the summit, marked by a large cairn, is reached.

The view from the ridge never fails to

impress: to the south lies a deep bowl containing Blea Water, overlooked by the slopes of High Street; to the north, Kidsty Pike rises above the wide cove of Riggindale. Golden eagles are often seen above Riggindale and the surrounding fells, though their eyrie is zealously guarded by members of the RSPB. *You can ease their vigil by keeping strictly to the path over Rough Crag during the breeding season (from mid-March to September).*

Continue along

the ridge and descend a little to a grassy col, Caspel Gate, where there is a small pool. Beyond this you engage an airy, twisting path ascending Long Stile, finally to reach the northern end of High Street **B**. The summit lies a couple of minutes south, and the simplest way of finding it in mist is to walk ahead (west) from the top of Long Stile until you intersect a dilapidated wall, and then follow this left (south) to the trig pillar.

From the summit, walk beside the wall to intercept a clear path that crosses a grassy link to Mardale Ill Bell: the right of way shown on the map across High Street does not exist on the ground. But, on a clear day, you can more or less head straight for Mardale Ill Bell. This last of the Kentmere west side fells forms a thumb of land separating Kentdale and Mardale, and

by moving north for a short distance from the main path as you reach the cairned summit, you discover a stunning view of Blea Water lying in its corrie below.

Continue with the path across Mardale Ill Bell, and follow its descent to Nan Bield Pass **C**, an ancient packhorse route crossing point. 'Nan' derives from the Welsh, and means a brook or a gorge, while 'bield' means a sheltered place. A small shelter sits in the middle of the narrow col.

Turn northwards from Nan Bield and begin a stony descent, the path casting about through rocky terrain, eventually to reach a cluster of low stone shelters beside Small Water. Stepping stones usually help you cross Small Water Beck providing delightful cascades as you follow its course towards Haweswater. But steadily the path moves away from the beck as it rounds the northern end of Harter Fell and finally descends to Mardale Head. ●

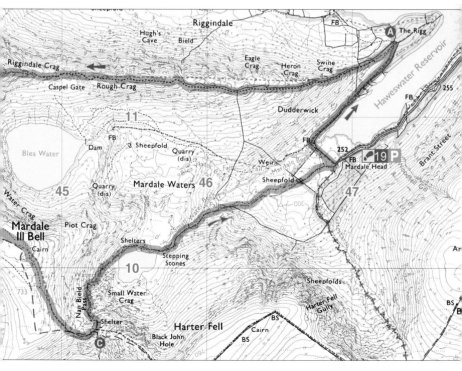

Place Fell

		GPS waypoints
Start	Patterdale	🥾 NY 396 159
Distance	7 miles (11.5km)	Ⓐ NY 408 158
Height gain	2,265 feet (690m)	Ⓑ NY 414 179
Approximate time	4 hours	Ⓒ NY 417 192
Parking	Opposite Patterdale Hotel (Pay and Display)	Ⓓ NY 398 162
Route terrain	Rough fell walking; stony tracks; steep ascent and descent	
Ordnance Survey maps	Landranger 90 (Penrith & Keswick), Explorer OL5 (The English Lakes – North-eastern area)	

Place Fell perches above Ullswater rather like a broody hen; the only significant fell to closely flank Patterdale. The main upthrust of summits to the west lean back from the dale, while north-east from Place Fell the fells diminish in size, although they are no less appealing. Throw in a rather spectacular shoreline on the east side of the lake along which to return, and an ascent of Place Fell suddenly rockets in popularity.

🥾 There is a convenient parking area opposite the **Patterdale Hotel,** and from this turn left along the road (it's safer if you cross it), and go past the odd-shaped **White Lion (toilets,** if needed, soon appear on the right).

'Patterdale' is the name given both to the valley and its principal community, described in Baddeley's *Guide to the English Lake District* as 'one of the most

Place Fell and Ullswater

charmingly situated in Britain, and in itself clean and comely.' Many villages, like Patterdale, were often presided over by one dominant family. In Patterdale it was the Mounseys, called the 'Kings of Patterdale', who lived at Patterdale Hall at the entrance to Grisedale.

The dale is especially pleasant, and is probably named after St Patrick, one of three eminent missionaries (along with St Ninian and St Kentigern) thought to have trawled this area on evangelical missions during the early years of the 5th century. Although there is a 'through-route' along Patterdale, it somehow retains a quiet aloofness, certainly when compared with the bustle of Ambleside and Windermere beyond the protective sleeping policeman of the Kirkstone Pass.

Stay on the main road, but shortly take the first turning on the left, a narrow lane that crosses Goldrill Beck, and

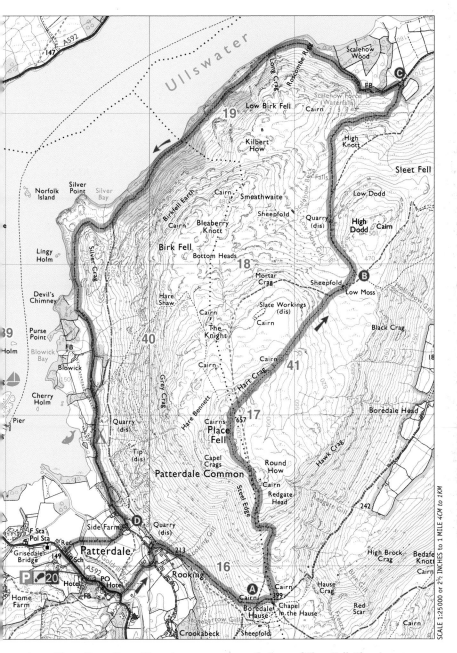

SCALE 1:25000 or 2½ INCHES to 1 MILE 4CM to 1KM

leads to the hamlet of Rooking. Walk past the houses to a gate on the right giving on to a path for 'Boredale Hause and Angle Tarn'.

A fine path, pitched in places, now slants in a south-easterly direction across the base of Place Fell. The views just seem to get better the more you ascend, and provide a welcome distraction from the effort, such as it is. To the south west there are particularly fine glimpses into Deepdale and Dovedale, while to the south the road slips past Brotherswater and climbs the Kirkstone Pass.

When the ascending path forks, keep left and gradually work a way up to the broad col known as Boredale Hause **Ⓐ**. Boredale is actually the next dale, running in a north-easterly direction, sandwiched between Place Fell and Beda Fell. Mark Richards, a latter-day doyen of Lakeland fell wandering explains that both Wordsworth and Wainwright made the mistake of assuming Boredale Hause had something to do with pigs, and hence used the spelling Boardale. In the ancient languages of Britain, the Scandinavian for pig was 'grise', and the Celtic-British was 'moch'. Boredale, he suggests, simply means 'the valley with a storehouse'.

In the hause you will find some stone ruins, said to be those of a chapel, but looking remarkably like a collapsed sheepfold. It would have been incredibly small, and some, including Dorothy Wordsworth, cast doubt on whether it was really a place of worship or simply a shelter, but a chapel here would have been logical given that the route was a busy crossing point between Patterdale and Martindale. It was Captain Luff of nearby Side Farm who showed the chapel to the Wordsworths, describing it as a place where the inhabitants of Martindale and Patterdale were accustomed to meet on Sabbath days. The chapel featured in Wordsworth's poem *The Excursion,* the story of a 'poor old man' overtaken by a storm while climbing onto the fell to collect peat, who used the chapel as a shelter.

At Boredale Hause you abandon the main trail, the Coast-to-Coast, which now wanders off in a southerly direction. Instead turn northwards and take to a clear, grassy path that ambles up onto the south ridge of Place Fell.

There is no doubt about the route. But console yourself with frequent stops to take in the spectacular scenery all around, and soon you find yourself at the trig pillar on the summit, flanked by a number of nooks and crannies in which to take a break. Another, nearby point holds a cairn, competing, probably vainly for the distinction of being the highest point.

The onward route lies in a north-easterly direction, passing a large pool and descending grassy slopes to a small depression at Low Moss **Ⓑ**. On passing a ruined sheepfold take a path on the left that strikes down a shallow valley targeting an area of slate spoil. A grassy path continues. When it forks, keep left, heading into the clutches of Scalehow Beck. Scalehow Force is not natural. What is now the Ullswater Outward Bound School was once a private mansion, the owner of which blasted the beck to create a waterfall in an effort to improve his view. Surprising in a way because the forward view of Sandwick Bay is really quite special.

The path leads down to a junction with another path, a bridleway **Ⓒ**, and here turn left, crossing Scalehow Beck by a footbridge and rejoicing in one of the finest and most popular paths in Lakeland. What makes it so popular is the steamer service on the lake, which brings walkers across to Howtown from where they can walk back behind Hallin Fell.

Flanking the north-west foot slopes of Place Fell, the path now heads for Silver Bay, and then speeds off southwards across Blowick meadows to reach Side Farm **Ⓓ**. Here turn right, between the farm buildings, and take a fine, broad track out to the valley road, re-crossing Goldrill Beck en route. When you reach the road, you may feel like diverting to the right to visit St Patrick's Church. But otherwise, turn left, and soon find yourself at the entrance to the car park. ●

Angle Tarn and Hayeswater

		GPS waypoints	
Start	Hartsop		NY 403 134
Distance	8 miles (12.5km)	Ⓐ	NY 399 144
Height gain	2,310 feet (705m)	Ⓑ	NY 407 157
Approximate time	4½ hours	Ⓒ	NY 418 145
Parking	Cow Bridge	Ⓓ	NY 433 129
Route terrain	Rough fell walking, but clear paths throughout		
Ordnance Survey maps	Landranger 90 (Penrith & Keswick), Explorer OL5 (The English Lakes – North-eastern area)		

Lording it over little known Bannerdale, Angletarn Pikes make an excellent objective, usually, as here, ascended from Patterdale. The agreeable visit to Angletarn Pikes and the nearby tarn is one of the finest walks from Patterdale. Here, it is extended to visit The Knott, and Hayeswater, a lovely lake set in a tranquil hollow below High Street and Gray Crag, and returns by way of the village of Hartsop, described by Molly Lefebure in Cumbrian Discovery *as '... quaint in the truest sense of that much abused word.'*

Begin from the Cow Bridge parking area to the north of Brothers Water. It was here, on the bridge that William Wordsworth sat in April 1802

Angletarn Pikes

as he and Dorothy walked towards Brothers Water and the Kirkstone Pass. His poem entitled *Written in March* was begun here and completed before the pair reached Kirkstone.

From this literary link, turn right

(away from the main road) and cross the bridge to reach two gates at a corner. Use either of these and bear immediately right above a fenceline and into light woodland (Low Wood), following a permissive path that threads a pleasant route through broad-leaved trees and finally emerges onto the valley road. A roadside verge with footpath leads, left, towards Bridgend, but, at Deepdale Bridge Ⓐ, cross to a gate giving onto a signposted bridleway (a broad farm track) heading towards the steep slopes of Dubhow Crag and Rake Crag. Cross Goldrill Beck, and shortly, at a track junction bear right through a gate. Within 100 yds, bear left onto an ascending stony path that now climbs steadily around Rake Crag to reach Boredale Hause Ⓑ.

At the hause there are the remains of a chapel (the so-called Chapel in the Hause) thought to date from the 13th century *(see Walk 20 for more information about the chapel).*

Look for a couple of cairns on the hause, near which you should move right to cross a small beck, ignoring all the paths going off to the left. Across the beck, the onward path, now part of the Northern Coast-to-Coast Walk is well-trodden and negotiates a series of twists and turns, ups and downs, and grassy knolls until, just as Angletarn Pikes first ease into view, there is a stunning view down to Brotherswater and the snail's trail of the Kirkstone Pass road.

The path now presses on easily until, with a final rocky flourish, you can leave it near the foot of the Pikes and ascend to the northernmost (and highest top). From the northern top, cross a brief boggy hollow to reach the southern summit and its view of Angle Tarn languishing in a broad hollow below. The view north, over the secluded sanctuary of Martindale and Bannerdale to the northern summits of the Pennines, is

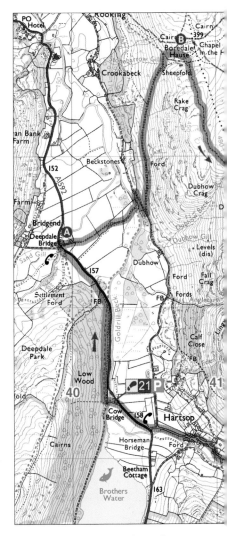

especially attractive on a frosty day, when the air is still – and worth lingering over. Nearby Angle Tarn is a tranquil and shapely expanse of water flecked with tiny islands, making this an ideal spot for a break.

Head down towards the tarn Ⓒ, where you will soon rejoin the main path left earlier, and follow it round Angle Tarn, climbing easily, with improving views, to a more level section as you approach Satura Crag. A short way on, you have to deal with a brief boggy section as the route crosses Prison Gill and Sulphury Gill.

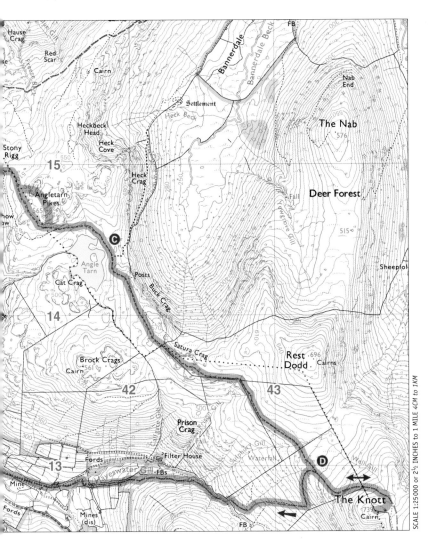

Ahead you see the great grass-flanked hollow that contains Hayeswater, rising to a superb ring of fells: Gray Crag on the right, across Thornthwaite Crag to High Street, the Straits of Riggindale, and the nearby summit of The Knott.

Once across Sulphury Gill you meet a path **D** ascending from Hayeswater. Calling for little extra effort, this continues to ascend finally to The Knott, from where the view of High Street in particular is one of the best.

From The Knott, go back down the Hayeswater path **D**, heading for the outflow of this small reservoir, from where a broad track leads, right, out of the valley and down to the tiny community of Hartsop, where a number of the blue-slate farmsteads still have spinning galleries and panelled cupboards, largely dating from around 1700.

Keep on through the car park at the approach to Hartsop, and on through the village to reach the main valley road (A592). Go forward along the roadside footpath to return to the Cow Bridge car park.

Helvellyn

		GPS waypoints	
Start	Patterdale		NY 396 159
Distance	8¼ miles (13.2km)	**A**	NY 383 156
Height gain	3,165 feet (965m)	**B**	NY 359 155
Approximate time	5 hours	**C**	NY 341 153
Parking	Opposite Patterdale Hotel (Pay and Display)	**D**	NY 389 159
Route terrain	A high mountain undertaking requiring scrambling ability. Some exposure on Striding Edge (mostly avoidable) and Swirral Edge (unavoidable). A good head for heights would be useful		
Ordnance Survey maps	Landranger 90 (Penrith & Keswick), Explorer OL5 (The English Lakes – North-eastern area)		

With the capacity both to inspire and to traumatise, this robust ascent of Helvellyn may well be the most popular high-level outing in the Lake District. The sheer persuasiveness of line attracts every fell-walking ambition sooner or later, and yet thwarts a few. Technically, the walk is not difficult, but the sense of exposure is in places a little intimidating, and before setting foot on Helvellyn itself, there is the minor issue of a brief downwards scramble that comes at the end of Striding Edge.

Turn left out of the car park, and opposite the **White Lion** go right onto a path climbing past **public toilets**. At the rear of an isolated building, leave the

track by turning left onto a path through bracken and heather. This leads to a gate giving onto open fellside.

A path climbs rockily for a short

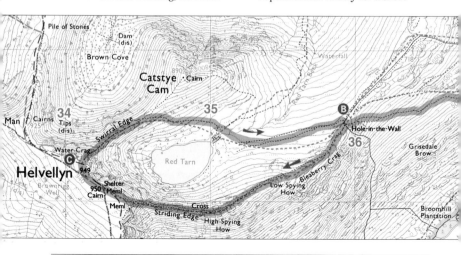

Helvellyn and Catstye Cam

way on, the path rejoins a wall and then leads to a gate. Pass through the gate and continue descending beside a wall to a couple of sheepfolds. There turn right through a gate, going down-field, past a barn to a surfaced track. Turn right to a gate 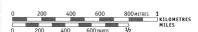, and then go left, soon crossing Grisedale Beck. Stay with the lane for a short distance further, until, at a bend, you can leave it, through a small gate, to ascend a steep pasture to another gate and wall.

while and then drops to a kissing-gate to the left of two other gates. Through this, follow the continuing wall, then climb to a horizontal path before descending gently to cross Hag Beck on stepping stones. The path continues easily, crossing the slopes of Glenamara Park and the steeper slopes below Thornhow End.

Follow the path as it runs alongside a wall bounding a pine plantation, and then maintain a level course when the wall drops away to the right. A short

Beyond the gate, the path, here joined by a path from Lanty's Tarn *(see Walk 12)* goes left and immediately forks. The lower branch sets off into Grisedale, while the higher, the route to be taken, begins the long and gradually rising approach to Striding Edge. As you climb, the view of Grisedale below becomes more and more impressive, brought abruptly to a halt by the crags of Nethermost Pike and Dollywaggon Pike that rise darkly at the head of the dale.

After a steady climb of about $1\frac{1}{4}$

SCALE 1:25 000 or 2½ INCHES to 1 MILE 4CM to 1KM

0	200	400	600	800 METRES	1
					KILOMETRES
					MILES
0	200	400	600 YARDS	½	

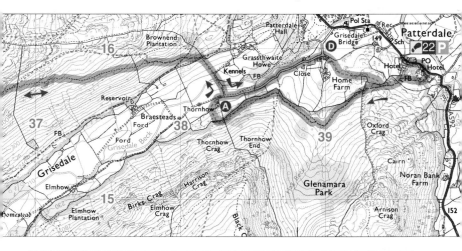

HELVELLYN ● 67

miles, the path spreads in a broad spill of loose stones that heralds the Hole-in-the-Wall **Ⓑ**, a stiled gap denoting the start of Striding Edge.

Beyond the stile, a few scattered rocks overlooking Grisedale offer a tempting and justifiable excuse for a break. It is here that Helvellyn and its neighbour Catstye Cam first come into view, above the basin that houses Red Tarn.

Striding Edge ripples along the left-hand edge of the hollow, and when ready, you follow an easy path heading towards it. *Those with no problem with heights and the ability to scramble a little, should consider leaving the main path, to follow the crest of the approaching ridge; it gives splendid views of Grisedale and St Sunday Crag. Eventually, both this approach and the path join at the start of the Edge proper. From this point, anyone who is uncomfortable in exposed situations should locate a path, low down on the Red Tarn side, by means of which you can circumvent all the difficulties of the Edge. The rest begin by working a way round the right edge of the rocky buttress immediately ahead, beyond which an assortment of precarious paths thread the rocks of Striding Edge. Those with a head for heights will follow the very crest of this splendid arête; anyone less confident can still enjoy Striding Edge, without too much commitment to exposed situations.* Escape routes generally lie down on the right (Red Tarn side), as you move towards Helvellyn.

Towards the end of the Edge, the path directs you, rather awkwardly for a stride or two, to the top of a short descending gully. This is most easily descended by facing inwards; there are plenty of good hand and foot holds, and the difficulties more imagined than real.

Once beyond this brief scramble, all that remains is the bulging shoulder of Helvellyn. A little more, easy scrambling awaits as the ongoing route climbs in two large steps (avoid going too far to the right) to the edge of the summit plateau. A nearby memorial, overlooking Red Tarn, commemorates Charles Gough of Manchester, and his faithful dog.

The summit of Helvellyn is something of an anticlimax. A cross-shelter provides comfort from most winds, and beyond it a short step up leads to the highest point, held in place by a lonely trig point.

Cross the top of the mountain, and locate a low cairn at the top of Swirral Edge **Ⓒ**. *The start of the descent is loose and exposed, and in winter a hazardous spot. The frequent use of hands and bottoms will assist passage down Swirral Edge, but haste is not a good idea here.*

Eventually, all the rockwork ends, as paths (on the Red Tarn side) combine to run ahead and up Catstye Cam. This sentinel is a good vantage point and worth the brief detour, from which you simply retrace your steps.

From the col between Catstye Cam and Swirral Edge, a branching path heads down, right, towards the outflowing stream of Red Tarn. A boggy interlude is experienced either side of the stream, before a slanting track runs left through tussocky grass, heading back to the Hole-in-the-Wall, from where you can simply retrace your outward steps to the surfaced lane in the valley.

At a T-junction **Ⓐ**, met with earlier in the walk, turn left and walk down the road until it makes a pronounced left turn. Here leave it by branching right onto a wide track **Ⓓ**. Shortly, leave the track at a waymark, pass through a kissing-gate, and follow a waymarked route across rough pasture to a high through-stile in a wall. Over the wall, rejoin the outward route. Turn left to follow it back to the start. ●

Great Dodd and Clough Head

		GPS waypoints	
Start	High Row, Dockray		NY 380 219
Distance	8¼ miles (13.2km)	**Ⓐ**	NY 373 221
Height gain	2,035 feet (620m)	**Ⓑ**	NY 348 211
Approximate time	4½ hours	**Ⓒ**	NY 350 227
Parking	High Row, very limited		
Route terrain	Rough moorland, pathless in places		
Ordnance Survey maps	Landranger 90 (Penrith & Keswick), Explorer OL5 (The English Lakes – North-eastern area)		

Lacking crag-bound corries, soaring arêtes and dramatic profiles, the sprawling, rounded, grassy domes of the Dodds do not seem to encourage closer acquaintance. They are formed from extensive lava flows, producing a bland plateau-like surface and wide-reaching moorlands.
Few walkers visit the Dodds for their own intrinsic qualities; yet in spite of a sameness about the scenery include excellent, easy walking, good views and a moorland solitude that is second to none. As this walk demonstrates, it may all seem straightforward, grassy, rounded fells, but the circuit is quite demanding, especially in its latter stages. The ability to navigate well is vital, and this walk should not be attempted in anything less than perfect visibility.

Clough Head

Begin the walk from High Row; there is very limited parking possibility here, so do park with consideration, or, better, add some distance to your walk by beginning from the free car park above Aira Force at NY 397 212. The road from Dockray runs along the north side of Aira Beck, and you should follow it to High Row.

At High Row, go through a gate to travel the old coach road that curls round the northern end of the Dodds to St John's in the Vale, but then leave this ancient thoroughfare after crossing Groove Beck by a bridge or ford, for a

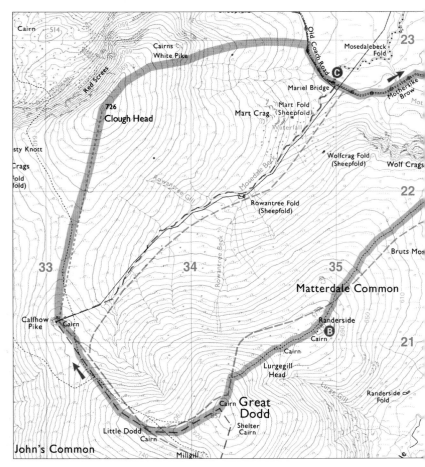

grassy track **Ⓐ** on the left. Ahead of you now, seemingly very far distant, rises the dome of Great Dodd, approached by a broad, ascending ridge of springy turf.

The rash of 'mosses' that stud the map hold a message – this is likely to be wet. And it is, often. Your main objective is the craggy lump of Randerside **Ⓑ**, on which there is a cairn, and beyond which you cross Lurgegill Head to begin the brief, cairned pull to Great Dodd summit, adorned by a cairn and a shelter a short distance away. If you want a break, then you need to visit the shelter even though it lies in the wrong direction, since it provides a better view and more shelter than the summit cairn.

The route now continues to Clough Head, a neat summit with a trig pillar. To get there you need to descend in a south-westerly direction from Great Dodd to follow a good path that leads to an intermediate pimple, Calfhow Pike, from where it is a straightforward pull up onto Clough Head. A grandstand view of Blencathra awaits, far across Greta's vale.

Beyond Clough Head, north and west, there is only craggy steepness. Escape lies to the east, down long grassy slopes of uneasy going, no path and no particular line other than one that intercepts the Old Coach Road close by Mariel Bridge **Ⓒ** – and since this ancient highway completely hems in Clough Head, you will, somewhere,

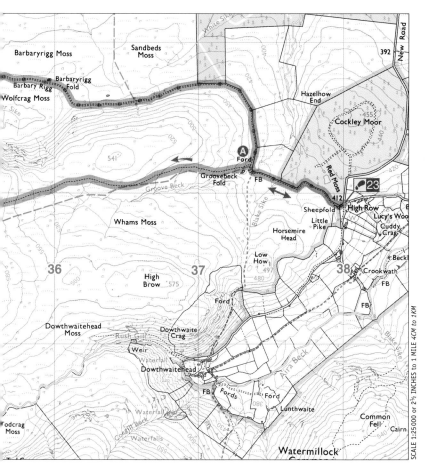

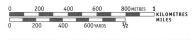

finally reach it, and not necessarily at Point **C**. When you do, turn right (east) and follow it back to High Row.

The Dodds from the slopes of Great Mell Fell

Kentmere Round

		GPS waypoints	
Start	Kentmere		NY 456 041
Distance	13 miles (21km)	**A**	NY 437 043
Height gain	3,805 feet (1,160m)	**B**	NY 431 101
Approximate time	7 hours	**C**	NY 452 096
Parking	Very limited parking at Kentmere, near church (only early arrivals will find space)	**D**	NY 473 069
		E	NY 477 049
Route terrain	High fell tops, plus numerous ascents and descents	**F**	NY 462 047
Ordnance Survey maps	Landranger 90 (Penrith & Keswick), Explorer OL7 (The English Lakes – South-eastern area)		

The Kentmere Horseshoe performs a splendid, extended loop around Kentmere Common and the Kent Valley, much of it at a high level. This is a long and demanding walk, and is best reserved for a summer's day and clear visibility.
A clockwise circuit gets four summits rattled off quickly, each involving ascent and descent that can be tiring towards the end of a day, leaving the relatively easier walking for the second half. It also has the advantage that if you are feeling weary by the time you reach Nan Bield Pass you can escape back to Kentmere at least having done six summits.

From St Cuthbert's Church, follow the road as it sets off for the Garburn Pass. The route is well signposted, and, as the metalled road comes to an end, go right on a signposted path. The track is then stony, but rises gently above the

Thornthwaite Crag

valley, with attractive glimpses of low fells, farms and cottages. Craggy outcrops dot the lower slopes of Yoke, on your right, indeed the area is known as the Crag Quarter.

There used to be a lake, or 'mere', just to the south of the church, where now there is nothing more than a swelling in the river, but the lake was only a shallow affair, and was drained in about 1840 to provide land for agriculture. Before then the vicar of Kirkby Thore, near Appleby-in-Westmorland, a renowned traveller, always with notebook in hand, had observed that the lake was about $\frac{1}{2}$ mile long and had a boat. It was apparently good for two kinds of trout, and hosted a large number of wild swans and duck.

In 1955, dredging along the river to gather diatomite for a processing plant at nearby Waterfoot uncovered what were believed to be two 10th-century, wooden, canoe-like boats, the best of which was later presented to the National Maritime Museum. These finds give a clear indication that the valley was inhabited from early times, and may well have been when the Romans were here, building their great highway across High Street.

Kentmere Hall, to the west of the village, is the oldest remaining structure, built around a 14th-century tunnel-vaulted pele tower. The adjoining farmhouse is a later addition, either 15th or 16th century. Neither is open to the public.

The hall used to be the home of a giant, Hugh Herd, the so-called Cork Lad of Kentmere, son of a nun from

MAP CONTINUES ON PAGE 74 ↓

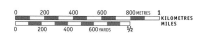

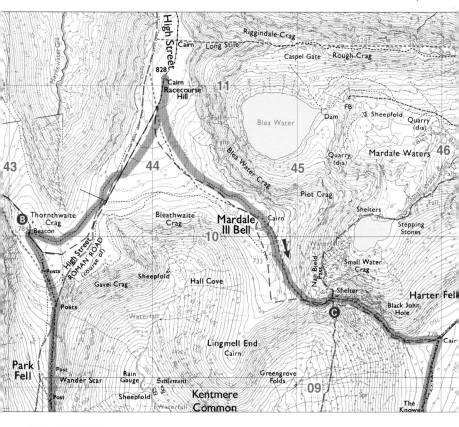

Furness who was cast out following the Dissolution. The giant was, not surprisingly, a champion wrestler, and served Edward VI during the time of the Border Troubles. The hall was also the home of Richard Gilpin, who has the notorious distinction of having killed the last wild boar in England, and of Bernard Gilpin (1517-83), a church reformer known as 'The Apostle of the North'.

A clear track runs up to the top of Garburn Pass **A**, there turning right through a gate to follow a grassy trod, never far from a long wall. When the wall changes direction, cross it and climb onto the broad end of Yoke, from where a path runs up to the summit. From Yoke the view is of mountains stacked on mountains, an endless flow rippling away in aerial perspective.

The next summit along the ridge is Ill Bell, a shapely cone recognisable from afar, and topped by a rough and craggy summit littered with cairns. A clear path above Star Crag and Rainsborrow Cove links Yoke and Ill Bell, and continues across the top of a steep drop into Over Cove and Kentmere Reservoir, to a miniature replica of Ill Bell, Froswick.

Thornthwaite Crag now awaits, pinned to the landscape by an enormous cairn. The long approach seems daunting, but easily succumbs to a steady plod. Again the excellent path continues its duty, branching left as it meets the line of the Roman road crossing the top of Gavel Crag, bound for High Street and beyond. Stroll on steadily and you will find the wall and low rock outcrops that mark the top of Thornthwaite Crag **B** to be a perfect nook for a timely break, possessing a fine view west over Stony Cove Pike and Red Screes, and south into the valley of Trout Beck.

A good path, setting off south of east and then swinging north-east takes you

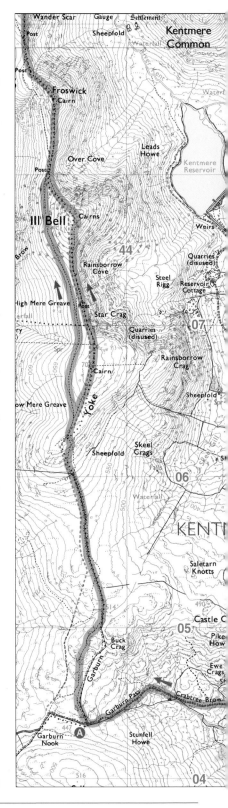

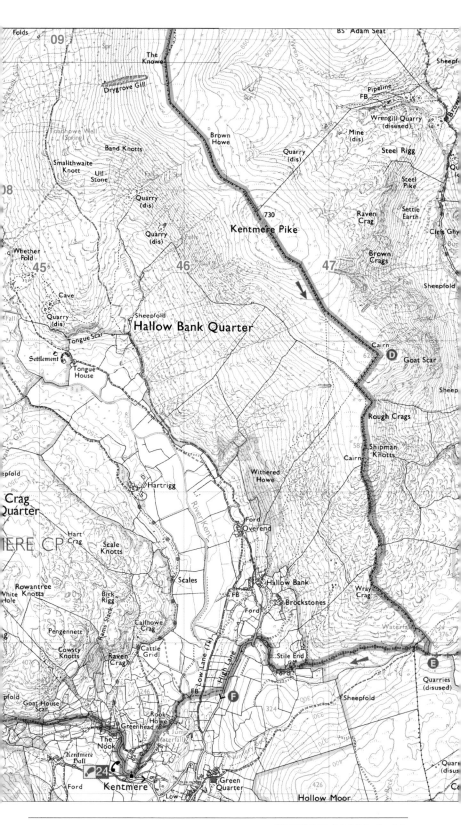

Ascending the Garburn Pass from Kentmere

to High Street along the course of the Roman road. The road, however, does not cross the summit of High Street, so leave it as you approach a wall, and accompany the wall to the trig pillar.

Retrace your steps beside the wall to continue on a clear path that crosses a grassy link to Mardale Ill Bell. On a clear day, you can head straight for Mardale Ill Bell from High Street. This last of the Kentmere west side fells forms a thumb of land separating Kentdale and Mardale, and by moving north for a short distance from the main path as you reach the cairned summit, you discover a stunning view of Blea Water nestling in its corrie below.

Continue with the path across Mardale Ill Bell, and down to Nan Bield Pass ⓒ, an ancient packhorse crossing point. 'Nan' derives from the Welsh, and means a 'brook' or a 'gorge', while 'bield' means a 'sheltered place'. A small shelter sits in the middle of the narrow col.

If you have had enough at this stage, turn right, down the pass and along a clear route back to Kentmere, picking up this route description as it descends from Shipman Knotts to meet the walled High Lane.

Otherwise, engage first gear, and begin the steady climb up onto Harter

Fell, actually nothing like as difficult or so long as it seems, rising in two easy stages to a large cairn not far from a fence and small boundary stone.

The fence, and later a wall, is now your guide to Kentmere Pike, speeding across springy turf to the few rocks that cap the disappointing summit; even the trig pillar hides from sight on the other side of the wall.

To press on to Shipman Knotts follow the fence to Goat Scar ⓓ, and then on to a wall that crosses the top of this rugged outlier, beyond which the wall leads you down to the top of the pass ⓔ linking Kentdale and Longsleddale. Turn right here, and follow a walled track down to Stile End, after which you soon connect with the Nan Bield route.

Now walk left along a walled lane (High Lane) until, at a signposted through-stile ⓕ, you can cross the wall and descend a field to Low Lane. Another stile accesses Low Lane, and directly ahead you can cross another field to a footbridge over the Kent. Turn left to follow an obvious path back to the church in Kentmere. If you miss the through-stile on High Lane, simply follow the lane down until you can turn sharply right, descending a narrow lane down to Low Bridge. ●

Hartsop Round

Start	Hartsop	GPS waypoints
Distance	8 miles (12.7km)	🖉 NY 403 134
Height gain	2,560 feet (780m)	Ⓐ NY 410 129
Approximate time	4½ hours	Ⓑ NY 426 103
Parking	Cow Bridge	Ⓒ NY 441 110
Route terrain	Rough, high-level mountain terrain	Ⓓ NY 426 127
Ordnance Survey maps	Landranger 90 (Penrith & Keswick), Explorer OL5 (The English Lakes – North-eastern area)	

The summits to the east of the Kirkstone Pass are hardly unfamiliar to visitors who use this high and in winter dangerous mountain pass. Yet, in any survey of the most fashionable Lakeland fells, it will be some time before anyone mentions this wild, lonely and amorphous area, where moorland stretches contrast with the beauty of verdant valleys; a soft, rounded hinterland with few savage intrusions; an area of harmonious companions. At its heart rises, High Street, made eternally famous by Roman navvies, who built a road across its spacious summit, linking their forts at Galava, near Ambleside, and Brocavum (Brougham), at the confluence of the Lowther and Eamont rivers.

🖉 From the car park, set off along the main road, heading towards Hartsop. There is a car park on the fell side of Hartsop village, but an approach along the road from Cow Bridge, turning left along the minor road for Hartsop, allows you to warm up gently and introduces you to the delights of this sheltered village, lying as it does in a side valley, off the main Patterdale valley.

The village of Hartsop is typical of many Lakeland fellside villages, and lies in a cul-de-sac, an attractive gathering in the folds of the fells of greystone-built cottages, some of which date from the 17th century, and a few still with the original spinning galleries that betray their origins as weavers'

cottages. Spinning galleries are a characteristic of Lakeland farm architecture, formed by carrying the roof beyond the wall, the space beneath the extended eaves providing useful storage space.

Hartsop was once within a vast hunting forest used for sport by kings and noblemen, and Hartsop's name may well derive from the deer that once extensively populated the area.

Beyond the village the second car park is encountered. Leave it by a gate and turn right, immediately to cross the nearby gill by a bridge Ⓐ. Turn left onto a good path running beside a wall. It soon swings right into Threshthwaite (pronounced 'Thresh'et') Glen and

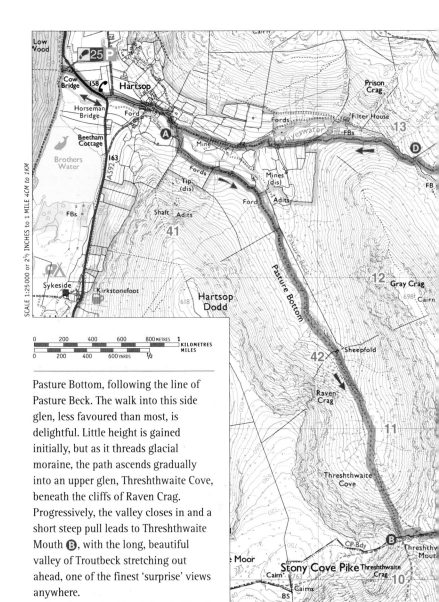

SCALE 1:25 000 or 2½ INCHES to 1 MILE 4CM to 1KM

Pasture Bottom, following the line of Pasture Beck. The walk into this side glen, less favoured than most, is delightful. Little height is gained initially, but as it threads glacial moraine, the path ascends gradually into an upper glen, Threshthwaite Cove, beneath the cliffs of Raven Crag. Progressively, the valley closes in and a short steep pull leads to Threshthwaite Mouth **B**, with the long, beautiful valley of Troutbeck stretching out ahead, one of the finest 'surprise' views anywhere.

A wall crossing Threshthwaite Mouth provides shelter from any winds breezing across the col, and ascends all the way to Thornthwaite Crag, a safe and reliable guide. *The section from the col requires care,* and not a little effort, but in it lies the key to a long, rewarding and lofty traverse. This energetic section is never as long as it seems, and as you ascend the view improves with every step, westward across Stony Cove Pike to Red Screes and the high central

mountains of Lakeland. A steady pull leads onto the upper slopes, and near the top the path bears right to run alongside a wall. The rarely visited Gray Crag lies off to the left (north), and it lends itself to a brief diversion to embrace its summit in the walk.

To say that the highest point of Thornthwaite Crag is marked by a cairn is a monumental understatement; no one is ever likely to forget the towering

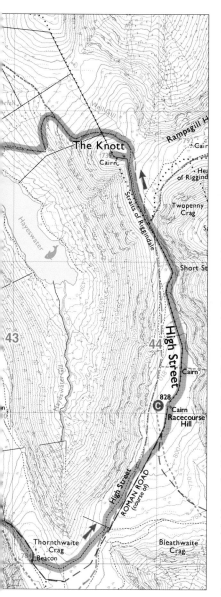

Pasture Bottom

trig marking the summit of this enormous whaleback is to leave the road after it adopts a straighter course, and move obliquely right to the wall which traverses the summit. This will lead you unerringly to the top C.

As a centre of attraction High Street has long served a popular purpose. Sir Clement Jones, youngest son of the vicar of Burneside, writing in 1955, mentions High Street, 'on whose flat top horse-racing and wrestling and athletic sports and all sorts of fun used to be enjoyed'. Even today, on some maps, the summit is called 'Racecourse Hill'.

Continue to follow the wall beyond High Street's summit plateau, where the ridge narrows abruptly and descends to the Straits of Riggindale, with a grand view down the valley of that name to the far eastern fells of Lakeland. And as you cross the Straits, follow the wall on your left, avoiding a path diverging right to Rampsgill Head, and in only a few minutes you reach The Knott, a fine, slightly conical hill. The path does not divert to this minor summit (although you can, and should), but continues instead around it to a wall, and a long, easy descent of grassy slopes, to the outflow of Hayeswater D. There is an enchanting loneliness about this spot, especially when autumn colours shade the fellsides.

From Hayeswater Dam it is a simple, descending stroll on a broad track back to Hartsop, and onward to Cow Bridge.

monolith standing in an angle in the wall.

From Thornthwaite Crag cross the wall, and set off on the line of a good path that starts off south of east around the headwall above Hayeswater Gill, and then curves north-eastwards to join the Roman road. The ancient road – the original 'High Street' – does not cross the summit of High Street fell, and the simplest way of ensuring you find the

Haweswater shore path

		GPS waypoints
Start	Burnbanks	
Distance	10 miles (16.3km)	✏ NY 508 161
Height gain	1,273 feet (388m)	Ⓐ NY 487 154
		Ⓑ NY 468 118
Approximate time	4½ hours	Ⓒ NY 479 118
Parking	Limited parking opposite telephone box. Please do not obstruct garages	Ⓓ NY 479 130
		Ⓔ NY 499 153
		Ⓕ NY 510 160
Route terrain	Entirely low level, on good tracks and paths throughout most of the route	
Ordnance Survey maps	Landranger 90 (Penrith & Keswick), Explorer OL5 (The English Lakes – North-eastern area)	

Although long stretches of this circular walk had been in use for some time – the north shore route is part of the Northern Coast-to-Coast Walk – only during 1995, was a complete link made possible in a partnership between the National Park Authority and what was then North West Water. Haweswater is the highest lake in the Lake District at 790 ft (240m), and the fourth deepest. The route concludes through Naddle Forest, a nature reserve and Site of Special Scientific Interest, where the red squirrel still survives; and passes other land managed by the Royal Society for the Protection of Birds, home to many rare species, including the golden eagle.

✏ Set off from Burnbanks by walking up a rough lane to the right of the telephone box, to pass cottages. The cottages were built to accommodate men working on the reservoir and dam, and although once falling into disrepair in recent times they have been restored. After the last of the cottages, go forward to a gate at which you enter light woodland. Follow a broad trail right and then left to a gate in a boundary fence.

Beyond the gate the track continues along the woodland boundary and across the base of open, craggy slopes clad in bracken, and dotted with hawthorn, rowan and gorse. The track climbs gently to a level section, where the reservoir, glimpsed through trees, comes into view along with, ahead on the right, the hanging valley of Fordingdale, through which flows Measand Beck.

The track continues uneventfully, but no less a joy to walk, accompanied either by a wall or a fence, and rising on the right to a conspicuous cairn on Four Stones Hill. A stretch of clear ground on the left allows a fine view up the length of Haweswater to the ring of summits at its head.

Near the ruins of a homestead, the broad track ends and becomes a narrow path, descending to cross streams before reaching the rocky gorge containing

Haweswater

Measand Beck . A bridge takes you over the beck, followed by a short rise to cross the low end of Sandhill Knotts before running on across more open fellside rising steeply on the right to the vast moorland reaches of High Raise and Long Grain.

Pleasant walking ensues on the approach to the great hollow of Whelter Bottom traversing steep slopes, undulating in delightful fashion. Finally, the path descends through bracken, beside which more collapsed stone walls leading down to the water's edge from the intake wall remind again that an isolated farming community once lived and worked in Mardale. A sturdy footbridge crosses Whelter Beck, cascading down a narrow ravine lined with holly bushes, rowan and alder. Above, the broken form of Whelter Crag rises steeply on the right, its grassy flanks often grazed by red deer.

Beyond the footbridge, the path heads for the intake wall before moving away to cross the snout of Birks Crag and Castle Crag, the site of an ancient British hill fort. The ongoing path now descends steeply as it approaches Riggindale, where it meanders through field enclosures, passing below a small wall-enclosed woodland. Rough Crag rises directly ahead and, as you round the edge of the woodland, the lower, craggy slopes of Kidsty Pike come into view. A sharp change of direction leads down to cross Randale Beck by a stone bridge, followed by a brief interlude of grassy terrain before a wooden footbridge across Riggindale Beck .

The path is then channelled between rows of low upright stones to reach a compact flight of steps and more upright stones leading to and through a small stand of larch. The way ahead now lies to the right of the prominent, wooded end of Rough Crag, known as The Rigg. Across this ridge, the path descends gently to find its way around the head of the lake, by footbridges and gates, to reach the car park at the roadhead.

At the northern edge of the car park go through a small gap in a low wall on to the signposted "Lakeshore Footpath: Burnbanks". Not far along this early leg

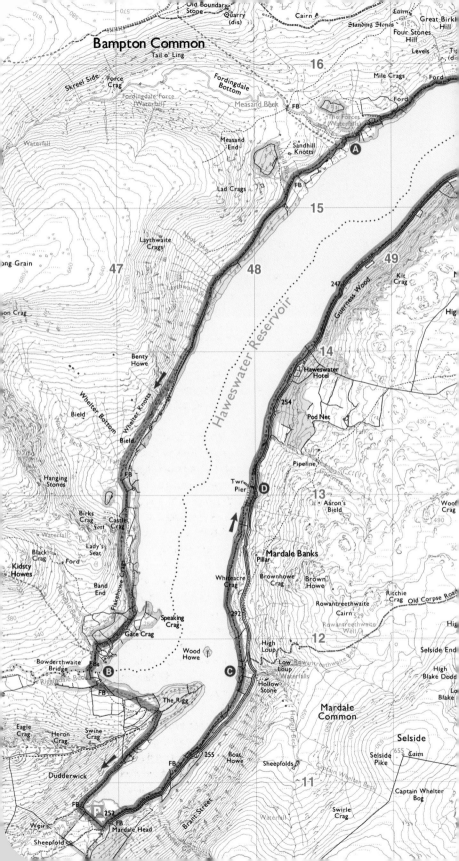

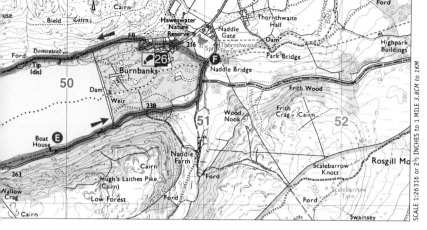

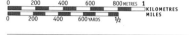

SCALE 1:26316 or 2½ INCHES to 1 MILE 3.8CM to 1KM

of the return journey, the path passes above the spot where the Dun Bull Hotel once stood, lost forever in a physical sense, but still of fond memory as a meeting place for shepherds and the people of these remote fells. In conditions of extreme drought, such as prevailed in 1984, the walls of the village lie exposed once more.

Throughout its entire length the path never strays far from the road wall, often pressing close up beside it, a visually limiting factor of no importance since all the views, and stunning they are, lie across the reservoir, into Riggindale, Whelter Bottom and, later, Fordingdale. For much of its course, the path undulates, dipping and diving through old enclosures to reach a footbridge spanning Hopgill Beck **C**.

Cross the bridge, and at a wall gap, follow the path ahead (signposted to Burnbanks). The path climbs out of the gill and then contours across slopes of bracken, hawthorn and holly. As the path approaches a reservoir control tower it enters woodland. There used to be a diversion here to take the path up to the wall, away from the vicinity of the tower, but this is less evident now, and walkers appear to be permitted to walk past the tower **D**, even though the concessionary path is still shown at a higher level on maps, as is the boundary of Access Land. The tower is the draw-

off point for the reservoir, and a building largely constructed from the remains of Mardale village church. A short way farther on, as the service track rises to the road, leave it by branching left back along the shore path.

Now you engage some delightful prime woodland, mainly birch, sycamore and beech, and encounter a number of places where the path crosses narrow ledges above steep drops to the reservoir. Frequently, as if afraid to leave its protection, the path clings to the wall, and, as a result, you pass by the **Haweswater Hotel** almost unaware of its existence. Elsewhere, the path meanders through the lowest edges of Guerness Wood, where raised tree roots can trip the unwary, or the weary.

With the dam in sight, the path weaves behind an old boathouse, before finally rising to the road at a gate **E**.

On the road, go left, and follow it round as far as Naddle Bridge **F**. Cross the bridge, and immediately turn left over a stone stile into oak woodland, a sylvan glade that for west-east Coast-to-Coast walkers effectively marks the end of Lakeland and the start of the limestone fringe en route for Kirkby Stephen. Within the woodland the path forks; either way will take you back to the edge of Burnbanks.

Wet Sleddale, Swindale and Mosedale

		GPS waypoints
Start	Wet Sleddale	📝 NY 555 114
Distance	12½ miles (17.5km)	Ⓐ NY 559 128
Height gain	1,540 feet (470m)	Ⓑ NY 537 144
Approximate time	5½ hours	Ⓒ NY 514 132
Parking	Wet Sleddale Reservoir	Ⓓ NY 506 100
Route terrain	Extreme moorland; hard surface tracks; minor road walking	Ⓔ NY 534 112
Ordnance Survey maps	Landranger 90 (Penrith & Keswick), Explorer OL5 (The English Lakes – North-eastern area)	

This long walk into a remote valley generates heaps of rugged and enjoyable moorland tramping around the ancient Ralfland Forest. Hard-surfaced service roads speed progress across some sections, while the shapely landscapes of Swindale and Mosedale expose the walker to the rarely visited folds of eastern Lakeland. This is a walk to be savoured leisurely, preferably on a good, clear day.

Although there is an ideal parking area at the south-eastern edge of Wet Sleddale Reservoir, if this is full, you can park, off-road and considerably, at Cooper's Green (NY 558 122), close by the footbridge spanning the embryonic River Lowther. In any case, you have to walk the road between the two points.

📝 Beyond the footbridge a gate gives access through a wall and onto a narrow lane. Turn right and follow the lane for 440 yds, until you rejoin the river, and then go left to follow a riverside path. Another 440 yds brings you to a service road Ⓐ that crosses the moors to Mardale. Turn left along this, striding freely and quickly with views of the hamlet of Keld and then of Shap Abbey *(see Walk 9)*. When you intercept the lane from Keld, go left bound for Tailbert Farm.

Just as you reach the first enclosed pasture of Tailbert, leave the road for an initially stony track Ⓑ cutting across the hillside. The track soon deteriorates into a less distinct grassy trod, leading on across the gorse and bracken flanks of Dog Hill, where Swindale eases into view below. The valley curves progressively southwards to an abrupt end, where a corpse road from Mardale enters the valley en route for Shap.

When you reach the valley bottom, there is a choice of a ford and stepping stones or a nearby bridge Ⓒ; both put you on the valley road. Turn left and walk to Swindale Head.

Go through a series of gates at Swindale Head and onto a bridleway for Mosedale, heading into the end of the dale where the fellsides rise steeply to Selside Pike and Swindale Common.

Wet Sleddale

The valley was bought from the Lowther Estate by the then National Water Board who drew up plans to flood the dale; thankfully the outbreak of the Second World War put a stop to the plans, but not before the chapel and school at Truss Gap were demolished.

Above the dale head, Mosedale Beck flows through a shallow, V-shaped moorland valley before plummeting into Swindale Forces. Nearby Hobgrumble Gill fills a dark gash in the cliff face, formed by waters seeping from a high corrie on Selside Pike. The streams combine amid glacial moraine to produce Swindale Beck, a bright treat in a sombre craggy dale.

Mosedale and Hobgrumble corrie are both hanging valleys, fashioned by the weight of ice that ground away at the sediments and rocks of the main valley floor. This whole region is populated by red deer that roam freely across the moors; pass this way in autumn and you will hear the bellowing of stags at the rut. Other than on foot or horseback there is no way through Swindale. The sense of remoteness is supreme.

Here, after the Romans had returned to sunnier climes, the Vikings came. Old maps show the name 'Thengeheved' below Gouther Crag on the south side of the dale. This was an ancient meeting place of Viking chiefs who would gather beneath the crag to settle the affairs of their communities. There is another in Little Langdale, but even more are surely lost to posterity. Now those same cliffs shelter peregrine, buzzard and winter flocks of travel-weary fieldfare, mistle thrush, redwing and brambling.

A walled track leads to a final building on the left, just beyond which it forks. Branch left. Beyond a final gate the ongoing track winds through moraine giving onto a grassy path that continues to take the route into Mosedale, winding upwards through the rocky outcrops of Selside Pike. The higher the path goes, the less distinct does it seem as it continues across open moorland to meet a fence at Swine Gill. Pass through a gate and press on to a nearby dilapidated building and a collapsed wall.

Follow the wall until a footbridge comes into view down on the left spanning Mosedale Beck. Stay on the path until you encounter a vehicle track cutting down to the bridge, known locally as Bog Bridge **Ⓓ**, and with good reason. On the other side, more tracks climb onto a broad ridge, rising to meet a fence and gate. Beyond this, a conspicuous grassy track climbs farther. When this forks, branch right. To the south-west, the distant Mosedale Cottage, surrounded by a stand of trees, lies midway between Swindale and Longsleddale, and is a forlorn spot below the spoil of the disused Mosedale Quarry.

Leaving this empty quarter, the walk climbs into Wet Sleddale, before beginning a long, easy descent just as the reservoir comes into view. After a second stile **Ⓔ**, just north-west of

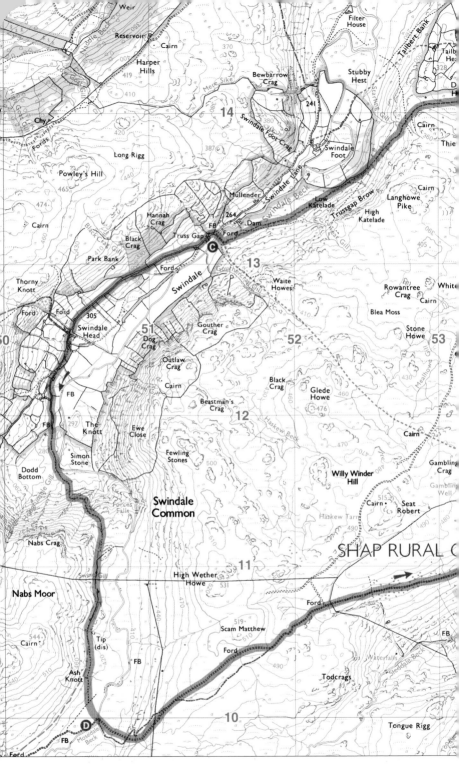

Sleddale Hall, turn right down zigzags that take you to the isolated farmstead at Sleddale Hall.

Sleddale Hall was the unlikely setting for the 1986 cult film classic *Withnail and I*, starring Richard E. Grant in his

first film role, and Paul McGann, who made his name in the BBC serial *The Monocled Mutineer,* and for briefly portraying the eighth 'Doctor Who' in the television movie.

Withnail and I, features two 'resting' actors, fed up with damp, cold piles of washing-up, mad drug dealers and psychotic Irishmen, they decide to leave their squalid Camden flat for an idyllic holiday in the countryside. But when they get there it rains non-stop, there's no food, and their basic survival skills are virtually non-existent. Wet Sleddale was perfectly type cast, and Sleddale Hall, which dates from the 18th century, became Crow Cragg in the film. Descend from Sleddale Hall to cross Sleddale Beck and then follow a clear track along the south side of the reservoir back to the parking area. ●

Loadpot Hill to High Raise

		GPS waypoints
Start	Burnbanks	🖊 NY 508 161
Distance	14½ miles (23.5km)	**Ⓐ** NY 487 154
Height gain	3,280 feet (1,000m)	**Ⓑ** NY 479 164
Approximate time	7½ hours	**Ⓒ** NY 456 181
Parking	Limited parking opposite telephone box. Please do not obstruct garages	**Ⓓ** NY 445 131
		Ⓔ NY 468 119
Route terrain	Exposed moorland mountain tops; good track alongside Haweswater	
Ordnance Survey maps	Landranger 90 (Penrith & Keswick), Explorer OL5 (The English Lakes – North-eastern area)	

Sandwiched between the long valleys of Martindale and Mardale, the grassy pudding-shaped fells that roll northwards from High Raise probably receive far fewer walkers than any other group of Lakeland fells. On a fine day, walkers on the Northern Coast-to-Coast Walk may cross them as an alternative to a low-level passage along the western shore of Haweswater. Otherwise, their only visitors will be ardent peak-baggers, solitude-seekers and the idly curious.
The whole range is traversed by the Roman road, High Street. That alone commends interest, but if you enjoy moorland wandering, and can cope with the inevitable diversions to avoid sporadic peat hags and boggy depressions, then the Loadpot Hill-High Raise ridge deserves your attention; it is a long walk but not unduly difficult.

The walk starts in the village of Burnbanks, built in 1929 to house construction workers building the Haweswater Reservoir and Dam. For a long time, Burnbanks was a sad sight – many of its houses demolished or derelict and an air of fateful resignation lying upon it like a sheen of abandonment. But then came redevelopment and builders and a whole new lease of life for this rather appealing settlement.

🖊 As you enter the village a surfaced track starts off on the right, past the telephone box, and this is the way to go.

Follow the track past cottages and out of the village, to enter the edge of woodland, wherein the path bends right and then left to a gate in an upper boundary fence. A broad track now runs beside the plantation, and accompanies either a wall or fence (on the left) across the base of low brackeny hills.

On the far side of the reservoir, the wooded slopes of Naddle Forest rise to a minor top, Hugh's Laithes Pike, which is said to mark the last resting place of a local ne'er-do-good, Jimmie Lowther, who broke his neck steeple chasing while drunk – an early case of drunken driving!

You need follow the broad track only as far as the narrow rocky gorge of Measand Beck 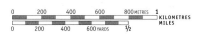. By then the track has lost weight and is now just a path leading to a bridge over the beck. Here, and higher up, Measand Beck puts on a turbulent display of cascades, known as The Forces, which in pre-reservoir days developed an enormous fan of gravel and boulders that almost reached the far side of the valley.

Having crossed Measand Beck, leave the main path and turn immediately right, climbing through bracken to follow the line of the beck to another bridge. Here you are at the entrance to the hanging valley of Fordingdale, one of Lakeland's almost forgotten dales, but well worth exploring.

Having crossed the second bridge, the way becomes less pronounced. Continue not up the dale but along the line of a tributary of Measand Beck (west of north) to a low col, east of Low Kop, where the remains of an old quarry **B** and a building tell of more toilsome

times. From the quarry a clear track leads westwards above the rim of Fordingdale to the southernmost of Wether Hill's two summits.

To the north rises Loadpot Hill. You can reach it more directly from Burnbanks, via the lonely valley of Cawdale, but inflowing tributaries and associated boggy going makes this an unappetising prospect. Wether Hill and Loadpot Hill, however, are linked by a good path passing the remains of Lowther House, a shooters' lodge. It is known that in days gone by Lady Lonsdale was accustomed to drive in her carriage to Lowther House for lunch. For a long time all that remained was a tall chimney, but that, too, has now succumbed.

Loadpot Hill carries a trig pillar **C**, with a small cairn and boundary stone a short distance away. From it you retrace your steps to Wether Hill, to begin a long, gently undulating stroll to High Raise, accompanied, at various distances, by a wire fence and a wall.

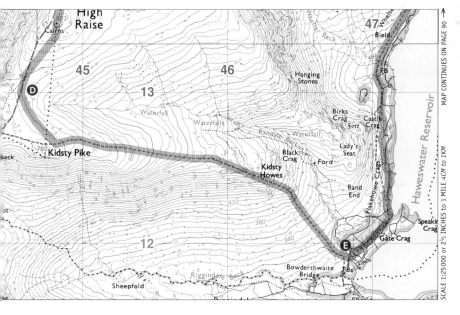

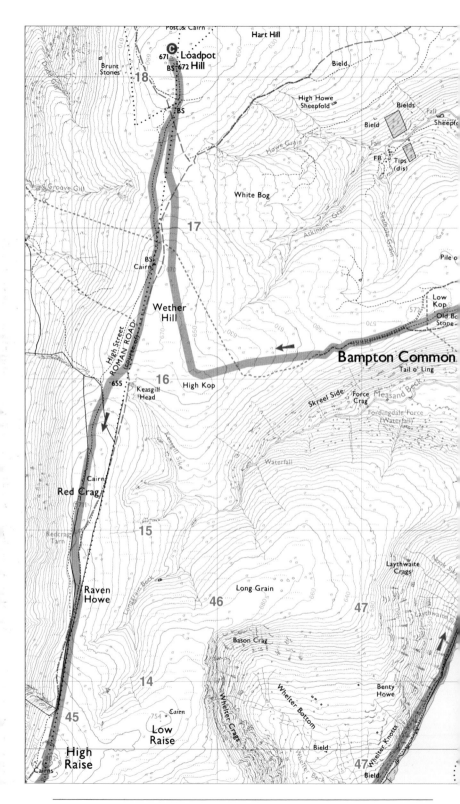

You traverse a few minor bumps, Red Crag and Raven Howe, before finally easing upwards to High Raise, on which a spread of rocks and stones has been gathered into a large cairn-shelter.

From High Raise keep following the Roman road across a shallow col **D** onto the stony edge of Rampsgill Head, before heading south-east to Kidsty Pike. Now a long, easy descent eastwards leads to Kidsty Howes. Here the path steepens and changes direction, as it drops to Riggindale Beck. As you approach the valley bottom you can bear left to a stone bridge spanning Randale Beck **E**. A brief climb takes you to the edge of a plantation. With this on your left, wander through derelict field enclosures before engaging the delightful, undulating traverse to the wide hollow of Whelter Bottom, from where you simply follow the Northern Coast-to-Coast route, a good, clear path all the way, back to Measand Beck and Burnbanks.

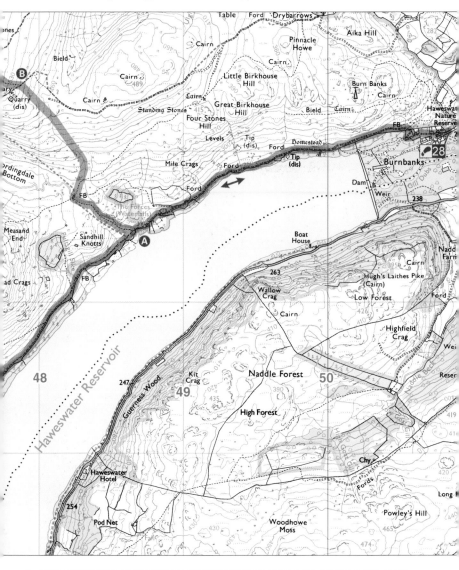

Further Information

Safety on the Hills

The hills, mountains and moorlands of Britain, though of modest height compared with those in many other countries, need to be treated with respect. Friendly and inviting in good weather, they can quickly be transformed into wet, misty, windswept and potentially dangerous areas of wilderness in bad weather. Even on an outwardly fine and settled summer day, conditions can rapidly deteriorate at high altitudes and, in winter, even more so.

Therefore it is advisable to always take both warm and waterproof clothing, sufficient nourishing food, a hot drink, first-aid kit, torch and whistle. Wear suitable footwear, such as strong walking-boots or shoes that give a good grip over rocky terrain and on slippery slopes. Try to obtain a local weather forecast and bear it in mind before you start. Do not be afraid to abandon your proposed route and return to your starting point in the event of a sudden and unexpected deterioration in the weather. Do not go alone and allow enough time to finish the walk well before nightfall.

Most of the walks described in this book do not venture into remote wilderness areas and will be safe to do, given due care and respect, at any time of year in all but the most unreasonable weather. Indeed, a crisp, fine winter day often provides perfect walk-ing conditions, with firm ground underfoot and a clarity that is not possible to achieve in the other seasons of the year. A few walks, however, are suitable only for reasonably fit and experienced hill walkers able to use a compass and should definitely not be tackled by anyone else during the winter months or in bad weather, especially high winds and mist. These are indicated in the general description that precedes each of the walks.

Walkers and the Law

The Countryside and Rights of Way Act (CRoW Act 2000) extends the rights of access previously enjoyed by walkers in England and Wales. Implementation of these rights began on 19 September 2004. The Act amends existing legislation and for the first time provides access on foot to certain types of land – defined as mountain, moor, heath, down and registered common land.

Where You Can Go
Rights of Way
Prior to the introduction of the CRoW Act, walkers could only legally access the countryside along public rights of way. These are either 'footpaths' (for walkers only) or 'bridleways' (for walkers, riders on horseback and pedal cyclists). A third category called 'Byways open to all traffic' (BOATs), is used by motorised vehicles as well as those using non-mechanised transport. Mainly they are green lanes, farm and estate roads, although occasionally they will be found crossing mountainous area.

Rights of way are marked on Ordnance Survey maps. Look for the green broken lines on the Explorer maps, or the red dashed lines on Landranger maps.

The term 'right of way' means exactly what it says. It gives a right of passage over what, for the most part, is private land. Under pre-CRoW legislation walkers were required to keep to the line of the right of way and not stray onto land on either side. If you did inadvertently wander off the right of way, either because of faulty map reading or because the route was not clearly indicated on the ground, you were technically trespassing.

Local authorities have a legal obligation to ensure that rights of way are kept clear and free of obstruction, and are signposted where they leave metalled roads. The duty of local authorities to install signposts extends to the placing of signs along a path or way, but only where the authority considers it necessary to have a signpost or waymark to assist persons unfamiliar with the locality.

Countryside Access Charter

Your rights of way are:

- public footpaths – on foot only. Sometimes waymarked in yellow
- bridleways – on foot, horseback and pedal cycle. Sometimes waymarked in blue
- byways (usually old roads), most 'roads used as public paths' and, of course, public roads – all traffic has the right of way

Use maps, signs and waymarks to check rights of way. Ordnance Survey Explorer and Landranger maps show most public rights of way

On rights of way you can:

- take a pram, pushchair or wheelchair if practicable
- take a dog (on a lead or under close control)
- take a short route round an illegal obstruction or remove it sufficiently to get past

You have a right to go for recreation to:

- public parks and open spaces – on foot
- most commons near older towns and cities – on foot and sometimes on horseback
- private land where the owner has a formal agreement with the local authority

In addition you can use the following by local or established custom or consent, but ask for advice if you are unsure:

- many areas of open country, such as moorland, fell and coastal areas, especially those in the care of the National Trust, and some commons
- some woods and forests, especially those owned by the Forestry Commission
- country parks and picnic sites
- most beaches
- canal towpaths
- some private paths and tracks Consent sometimes extends to horse-riding and cycling

For your information:

- county councils and London boroughs maintain and record rights of way, and register commons
- obstructions, dangerous animals, harassment and misleading signs on rights of way are illegal and you should report them to the county council
- paths across fields can be ploughed, but must normally be reinstated within two weeks
- landowners can require you to leave land to which you have no right of access
- motor vehicles are normally permitted only on roads, byways and some 'roads used as public paths'

Further Information

The New Access Rights

Access Land

As well as being able to walk on existing rights of way, under the new legislation you now have access to large areas of open land. You can of course continue to use rights of way footpaths to cross this land, but the main difference is that you can now lawfully leave the path and wander at will, but only in areas designated as access land.

Where to Walk

Areas now covered by the new access rights – Access Land – are shown on Ordnance Survey Explorer maps bearing the access land symbol on the front cover.

'Access Land' is shown on Ordnance Survey maps by a light yellow tint surrounded by a pale orange border. New orange coloured 'i' symbols on the maps will show the location of permanent access information boards installed by the access authorities.

Restrictions

The right to walk on access land may lawfully be restricted by landowners. Landowners can, for any reason, restrict access for up to 28 days in any year. They cannot however close the land:

- on bank holidays;
- for more than four Saturdays and Sundays in a year;

- on any Saturday from 1 June to 11 August; or
- on any Sunday from 1 June to the end of September.

They have to provide local authorities with five working days' notice before the date of closure unless the land involved is an area of less than five hectares or the closure is for less than four hours. In these cases land-owners only need to provide two hours' notice.

Whatever restrictions are put into place on access land they have no effect on existing rights of way, and you can continue to walk on them.

Dogs

Dogs can be taken on access land, but must be kept on leads of two metres or less between 1 March and 31 July, and at all times where they are near livestock. In addition landowners may impose a ban on all dogs from fields where lambing takes place for up to six weeks in any year. Dogs may be banned from moorland used for grouse shooting and breeding for up to five years.

In the main, walkers following the routes in this book will continue to follow existing rights of way, but a knowledge and understanding of the law as it affects walkers, plus the ability to distinguish access land marked on the maps, will enable anyone who wishes to depart from paths that cross access land either to take a shortcut, to enjoy a view or to explore.

General Obstructions

Obstructions can sometimes cause a problem on a walk and the most common of these is where the path across a field has been ploughed over. It is legal for a farmer to plough up a path provided that it is restored within two weeks. This does not always happen and you are faced with the dilemma of following the line of the path, even if this means treading on crops, or walking round the edge of the field. Although the later course of action seems the most sensible, it does mean that you would be trespassing.

Other obstructions can vary from overhanging vegetation to wire fences across the path, locked gates or even a cattle feeder on the path.

Use common sense. If you can get round the obstruction without causing damage, do so. Otherwise only remove as much of the obstruction as is necessary to secure passage.

If the right of way is blocked and cannot be followed, there is a long-standing view that in such circumstances there is a right to deviate, but this cannot wholly be relied on. Although it is accepted in law that highways (and that includes rights of way) are for the public service, and if the usual track is impassable, it is for the general good that people should be entitled to pass into another line. However, this should not be taken as indicating a right to deviate whenever a way becomes impassable. If in doubt, retreat.

Report obstructions to the local authority and/or the Ramblers' Association.

Useful Organisations

Council for National Parks
6/7 Barnard Mews,
London SW11 1QU
Tel. 020 7924 4077
www.cnp.org.uk

Council for the Protection of Rural England (CPRE)
128 Southwark Street,
London SE1 0SW
Tel. 020 7981 2800
www.cpre.org.uk

Cumbria Tourist Board
Ashleigh, Holly Road,
Bowness-on-Windermere,
Cumbria
LA23 2AQ
Tel. 015394 44444
www.golakes.co.uk

Forestry Commission
Silvan House, 231 Corstorphine Road,
Edinburgh EH12 7AT
Tel. 0131 334 0303
www.forestry.gov.uk

Friends of the Lake District
Murley Moss, Oxenholme Road,
Kendal, Cumbria LA9 7SS
Tel. 01539 720788
www.fld.org.uk

**Lake District National Park Authority
information centres** *(*not open all year)*:
*Ambleside: 015394 32729
*Bowness Bay: 015394 42895
*Broughton-in-Furness: 01229 716115
*Coniston: 015394 41533
*Glenridding: 017684 82414
*Grasmere: 015394 35245
*Hawkshead: 015394 36525
Keswick: 017687 72645
*Pooley Bridge: 017684 86530
*Waterhead: 015394 32729

Lake District National Park Visitor Centre
Brockhole, Windermere, Cumbria LA23 1LJ
Tel. 015394 46601
www.lake-district.gov.uk

Long Distance Walkers' Association
www.ldwa.org.uk

National Trust
Membership and general enquiries:
PO Box 39, Warrington, WA5 7WD
Tel. 0870 458 4000
North West Regional Office:
The Hollens, Grasmere, Ambleside,
Cumbria LA22 9QZ
Tel. 08706 095391
www.nationaltrust.org.uk

Natural England
1 East Parade, Sheffield, S1 2ET
Tel. 0114 241 8920
www.naturalengland.org.uk

Ordnance Survey
Romsey Road, Maybush,
Southampton SO16 4GU
Tel. 08456 05 05 05 (Lo-call)
www.ordnancesurvey.co.uk

Ramblers' Association
2nd Floor, Camelford House,
87–90 Albert Embankment,
London SE1 7TW

Tel. 020 7339 8500
www.ramblers.org.uk

Youth Hostels Association
Trevelyan House, Dimple Road,
Matlock, Derbyshire
DE4 3YH
Tel. 01629 592600
www.yha.org.uk

 Ordnance Survey maps of the Lake District

The Lake District is covered by Ordnance Survey 1:50 000 ($1\frac{1}{4}$ inches to 1 mile or 2cm to 1km) scale Landranger map sheets 85, 86, 89, 90, 91, 96, 97 and 98. These all-purpose maps are packed with information to help you explore the area. Viewpoints, picnic sites, places of interest and caravan and camping sites are shown, as well as public rights of way information such as footpaths and bridleways.

To examine the Lake District in more detail, and especially if you are planning walks, Ordnance Survey Explorer maps at 1:25 000 ($2\frac{1}{2}$ inches to 1 mile or 4cm to 1km) scale are ideal. Four such maps cover the main Lake District National Park:

OL4 (The English Lakes –
    North-western area)
OL5 (The English Lakes –
    North-eastern area)
OL6 (The English Lakes –
    South-western area)
OL7 (The English Lakes –
    South-eastern area)

The Lake District area is also covered by Ordnance Survey touring map number 3, at 1 inch to $1\frac{1}{2}$ miles or 1cm to 1km (1:100 000) scale, which includes useful guide information on the reverse.

To get to the Lake District, use the Ordnance Survey Travel Map-Route at 1:625 000 (1 inch to 10 miles or 4cm to 25km) scale or OS Travel Map-Road 4 (Northern England) at 1:250 000 (1 inch to 4 miles or 1cm to 2.5km) scale.

Ordnance Survey maps and guides are available from most booksellers, stationers and newsagents.